OUTWARD BOUND
MAP AND COMPASS
HANDBOOK

Also available
Outward Bound First Aid Handbook

OUTWARD BOUND
MAP AND COMPASS
HANDBOOK

Glenn Randall

With additional text by John Hinde

WARD LOCK

A WARD LOCK BOOK
First published in the UK in 1994
by Ward Lock
Villiers House
41/47 Strand
London WC2N 5JE

A Cassell Imprint

Distributed in Australia by
Capricorn Link (Australia) Pty Ltd
2/13 Carrington Road, Castle Hill, NSW 2154

British Library Cataloguing-in-Publication data
A catalogue record for this book is available from the British Library

ISBN 0-7063-7284-0

Line illustrations: Ben Cracknell
Front cover photograph: Stephen Whitehorne
Back cover photograph: Mark Allen Publishing

Typesetting and design: Ben Cracknell
Printed and bound in Finland by Werner Söderström Oy

Contents

About Outward Bound®

The Outward Bound Trust provides high-quality courses in a range of exciting outdoor activities. Our fully qualified instructors maintain the highest standards of tuition, and our safety record is second to none. Everyone who takes an Outward Bound course enjoys a rewarding and memorable experience, the benefits of which will last a lifetime.

Outward Bound courses have been available in Britain since 1941. The original courses were the outcome of a meeting between Kurt Hahn, the educator, with Lawrence Holt, the owner of a shipping line. The marriage of the worlds of education and business is a vital feature of the Outward Bound movement. The courses are both a valuable adjunct to formal education and an important part of career development.

From its beginnings in Britain the Outward Bound movement has spread throughout the world, with 38 centres in 23 countries.

A typical course in the UK lasts from one to three weeks and may be based at one of our five national centres or may take the form of an expeditionary journey by foot or by sailing boat in a wilderness setting. We run courses for all age groups, from 14 to 70!

The Outward Bound Trust also works directly with industry in designing programmes to help companies through periods of change. This may involve developing leadership skills for young managers or assisting in building cohesive teams. The courses balance challenging outdoor tasks with reflection and review. They are specially designed so that participants can always translate what they gain from a course back to their working environment.

After an Outward Bound experience, people discover many positive attributes about themselves. They become more confident; they learn to share; to lead and to follow; to understand their own strengths and to work together as a group. By safeguarding each other, they form bonds of trust. They discover that many problems can be solved only with the co-operation of all members of a group.

To find out more about Outward Bound courses or to request a brochure, please contact us at the address below:

Outward Bound Trust
Head Office
Chestnut Field
Regent Place
Rugby CV21 2PJ

Tel (0788) 560423

Ian Fothergill
Director, Outward Bound Trust

Introduction

'It was 3 a.m. and our altitude was above 6100m (20 000ft). Mike Banks, Hugh Wiltshire and I were about to achieve the first British ascent of Mount McKinley, the highest summit in North America. We had already been repulsed twice: the first time retreating from a bivouac on an ice-slope at 5000m (16 400ft), which had been swept by powder snow avalanches throughout the night, secondly when we had to drag Has Oldham down 1000m (3330ft) after he suffered high altitude oedema above the Granite Ridge.

'It was the third attempt for Mike and me. Storms punctuated the unremitting cold. From our third camp at Kahiltna Pass we had to lie up for whole days: at the foot of the West Buttress ice-slope, and again at 5250m (17 200ft), when violent winds made travel foolhardy, and the noise of the tent flapping unbearable.

'We started at 7 p.m. during a lull, and climbed through midnight, across the glaciers to Denali Pass. My vapour-barrier double boots were huge and soft, made of micro-cellular rubber. It was vital to keep my crampons secure, and so I had to overtighten the straps. This had already caused third degree frostbite in my right big toe, but I did not find this out until 36 hours later. Abreast of the Archdeacon's Tower, I was in a bad way, sometimes staggering and often slurring my speech. I had plenty of glucose in my rucksack but I was too tired to take it off and undo the straps. Instead, I went down on my knees and slurped glucose tablets from the palm of Mike's outstretched eiderdown mitt. Two tablets, and I was OK for the next 50m (160ft), then stopped again. At Kahiltna Horn the lightening day seemed darker to me and I saw it with double vision. All these were symptoms of exhaustion hypothermia, but we knew very little about exposure in 1962.

'We took "glory pictures" of each other on the summit. I could see right down to the Muldrow Glacier over 3000m (10 000ft) below us, with fifty or a hundred spectacular mountains which we were only just in time to see. Within less than five minutes we watched clouds boil up all around us. We were swallowed up in greyness, seeing nothing through the mist except each other and about 5m (16ft) of iron-hard névé which our cramponed feet had barely scratched. Mike and Hugh might have planted red-flagged cane wands whilst I staggered up − I can't remember − but they were too far spaced across the emptiness to be of any use in finding our way down.

'We had to find our tent. It was the only haven between us and our seven friends at Kahiltna Pass, 8km (5 miles) away, and 3300m (10 800ft) below. As far as we knew there was nobody else in the whole Alaska Range. I could not help with the navigation because I was too far gone from lack of oxygen. I was placed in the middle of our three-man rope team to be "looked after". One went ahead with the compass, the other in the rear also with a compass, stopping frequently, checking the direction of our single file and keeping us right by shouting course corrections. Four hours later, still in cloud, we reached the tent, and melted ice on our Primus stoves to make tea. We had been going for 12 hours, and I owed my life to Mike and Hugh. Without a map and compass, the skill to use them, and at least one cool head to insist we should trust them, we might have wandered on the mountain for another day or longer, worsening our frostbite, hastening the deterioration of our already wasted bodies, and further reducing the chances of descending safely.'

John Hinde

Everyone who plays or works outdoors needs route-finding skills, though only a few, thankfully, will need them as urgently as we did. Day walkers and backpackers will find a map and compass useful for identifying landmarks, making the correct turn at path junctions, and estimating travel time even if they always follow established routes. Everyone who leaves those well-trodden ribbons of civilization will find route-finding tools essential. Cross-country skiers can easily find themselves in the same situation as the off-road summer hill-walker. Ski trails vanish with every snowfall. In the forest, with the surrounding peaks hidden by trees, a map and compass (and sometimes an altimeter) often provide the only practical means of route-finding. In open forests, meadows and above the tree line, ski tracks can drift over within minutes in high winds even if the sky is clear. Mountaineers travelling across glaciers and featureless snowfields become completely dependent on their map-and-compass skills (and foresight in marking their trail) whenever fog and storms move in. Sea-kayakers and canoeists crossing open water are equally dependent on route-finding skills.

If you read this book carefully, and (even more important) spend a few hours practising the skills it teaches, you will master route-finding the easy way, and save yourself many anxious moments.

After reading this book, you will know how to:

☑ create a mental image of a landscape while studying a map

☑ use a compass, by itself, to find your way there and back again

☑ combine map-reading and compass skills to identify a landmark, plot your course and determine your location

☑ use an altimeter to pinpoint your position

☑ avoid the most common route-finding errors

☑ use a whole array of easy navigation tricks that simplify walking in the outdoors.

1

How to read a contour map

Sometimes you can solve your navigational problems with just a good map and common sense, as John Hinde's experience proves.

'A few years ago, a friend and I were sea-kayaking along the inhospitable coast from Mallaig on the Sound of Sleat to Tarbet Bay on Loch Nevis. We had paddled downwind in a westerly Force 5, with cold rain falling from swollen clouds only 30m (100ft) overhead. It was essential that we reached Tarbet Bay, as our kayaks were full of expedition rations for a party near Swordland on Loch Morar. If we missed the isthmus, rugged hills would prevent us carrying over-laden rucksacks to them. What we could see of the coast through the rain and mist was a bit worrying, as heavy swells crashed on to the rocks and tiny beaches with steep crags and hillsides disappearing into the clouds above.

'We knew half our journey was completed when we turned right, and we found some shelter from the wind which had been on our tails, although there were still some nasty squalls and down-draughts from the hills. There were some bays with scattered ruins of crofts and other buildings, but in the thickening fog, it was hard to distinguish them.

'"Is that it?" Bill asked, an hour after we rounded the cape. He pointed through the swell and the murk to some buildings and a point beyond, which had all the credibility of a mirage. I had to agree that the bay looked vaguely right. Then Bill double-checked with the waterproofed map attached to the deck forward of his cockpit coaming. "That can't be it", he decided.

How did he reach that conclusion so quickly? In the fog we could only guess at the cove's outline and dimensions. Although we had been able to see snatches of the coastline as we paddled south south east, no other landmarks were now visible.

But Bill had landmarks in his head.

'"We've passed only two bays with ruins so far", he said. "This is the third. Tarbet Bay is still at least a kilometre ahead."'

That kind of navigating requires no great map-reading skills. It doesn't even demand use of a compass. What it does require is paying careful attention to the landscape around you. Raise your eyes from the ground (or sea) and really study your surroundings! That is the first key to successful navigating.

Being aware means looking back over your shoulder as well as forward. The world looks very different heading down the mountain from the way it did going up. Memorize the shape of the little pinnacle that marks the point where you joined the ridge. Remember the appearance of the fallen logs that mark where the path turns away from the forestry fence. You cannot count on your footprints to guide you when you return along the same route. A group of walkers could come along, miss the junction and walk half a kilometre up the hill before realizing their mistake. If you follow the main body of footprints – theirs – you will make the same error.

Paying attention to your watch can also help you to estimate your position. We knew that we generally paddled about 5km (3 miles) per hour. It had taken an hour and a quarter for us to paddle from Mallaig to the cape in the westerly wind. We knew we had not paddled any faster in the middle stretch of Loch Nevis. Even though the going had been easier, we could have looked at the map and, without measuring anything, known it was unlikely that we had reached Tarbet Bay in just one hour. We had checked the tide tables and knew that it was low water and neap tides an hour after we left Mallaig, so we had no tidal calculations to bother about.

Proper nautical charts should be used for sea-kayaking. As well as submarine depths and tides, they give some idea of land forms. An Ordnance Survey map would show the hillsides better; it would be possible, though not recommended, to use a basic *planimetric* map.

Planimetric maps show the world as if it were all on one plane. A typical road map is a good example. It always shows the ground as if the observer was directly overhead. That means a right angle on the ground (a road junction, for example) is always represented by a right angle on the map.

Equally important, 1cm (^{1}/$_2$in) on the map always represents a particular distance on the ground. That relationship is the map's *scale*. On a road atlas of Britain, the scale might be 4cm to every 10km (or 1in to 4 miles). On a map useful for walking, the scale might be 2 or 4cm to every kilometre (or 1in to ^{1}/$_2$ mile). The scale is usually expressed as a ratio: 1:50 000 for example, which means that 1cm on the map equals 50 000cm on the ground – in other words – 500m (or 1 in = 50 000in, i.e. 1390yd). On a 1:25 000, 4cm equals 1 000m, or 1km (or 1in = 25 000in, i.e. 694yd). As I explain in more detail later, most maps have a scale which shows graphically what distance on the map equals one kilometre or mile on the ground.

Planimetric maps, like most maps, also have a legend: a chart showing what the symbols used on the map mean. Some symbols are obvious: irregular blue splotches are typically lakes, for example. Others, such as a dashed line, can mean a four-wheel-drive track on one map and a path for walkers only on another. Knowing the symbol's meaning can prevent you from breathing a lot of exhaust fumes!'

Contours

Most interesting wilderness areas are not flat, and here you will need a contour or relief map.

Contour maps show the ups and downs of the terrain by means of *contour lines*. A contour line is a line on the map that represents

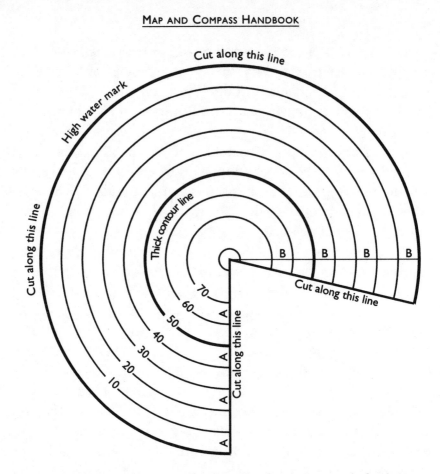

1.1 Cut along the marked lines, place line A over line B and tape securely. Set the cone you have just made point-up on a tabletop. If you would rather leave the book intact, cut out a copy of the drawing.

the same altitude throughout its length. It may duck into valleys and bulge out around ridges, but it still marks the same height. The line indicating the shore of a lake is a good example.

The easiest way to visualize the way contour lines relate to mountains and valleys is to build yourself a little conical island. You will find the materials in the form of figure 1.1.

First, cut along the outer edge of the figure, as indicated. Place line A above line B, tape securely, and put the resulting paper cone point-up on a tabletop. Looked at from the side, it should resemble a little volcano, with horizontal lines – contour lines – running

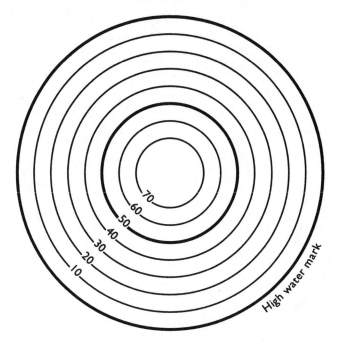

1.2 Representation of your paper cone on a contour map.

across it. Each line is at the same height above the table through-out its length. Similarly, each contour line is the same height above sea-level throughout its length. The height change from one line to the next is called the *vertical interval* or *contour interval*. On any given map, it is always the same.

Look at the cone from directly above, as if you were in an aircraft flying overhead. Notice how the contour lines form con-centric circles. The biggest circle is closest to the tabletop.

Successively smaller circles represent successively higher eleva-tions. This view from above shows your paper volcano, or island, in exactly the same way that a contour map would depict it. Figure 1.2 shows how your cone would be mapped.

This is the first principle of understanding contour maps. Concentric contour lines that form complete, closed paths, whether they constitute circles or some irregular shape, represent moun-tains and hills. Circular or semicircular depressions in the earth are represented by similar contours.

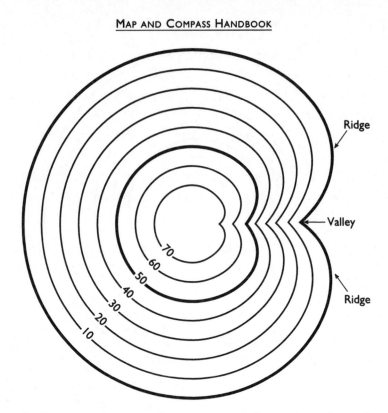

1.3 A contour map representation of your paper cone after you crease it to make a valley.

To understand how contour lines relate to valleys, look at your paper cone again. Press in slowly on one side of the cone near the bottom to create a valley. Crease the paper so the crease runs along the valley bottom. Now look down at the cone from directly overhead. Let it flatten out in your mind's eye, as if you were looking down at a map. Notice how the contours in the valley form 'V's whose sharp tips point to higher elevations. Figure 1.3 shows how your volcano-with-valley would be mapped.

This is the second principle of understanding relief maps. Contour lines in valleys form 'V's pointing to higher ground. Sometimes the 'V's are softened into 'U's, but the principle still holds.

Ridge contours resemble valley contours except that the contour lines generally form 'U's and always point to *lower* ground. In figure 1.3, arrows mark the broad ridges that enclose the valley. The presence of a blue line indicating a stream is a sure sign of a valley, but not all valleys have streams. To be certain whether a group of contours represents a valley or a ridge, you need to look for the heights marked on the map to determine which way the land is sloping.

Look at figure 1.4. The thin contour lines are called *intermediate contours*. The darker, thicker contour lines are called *index contours*.

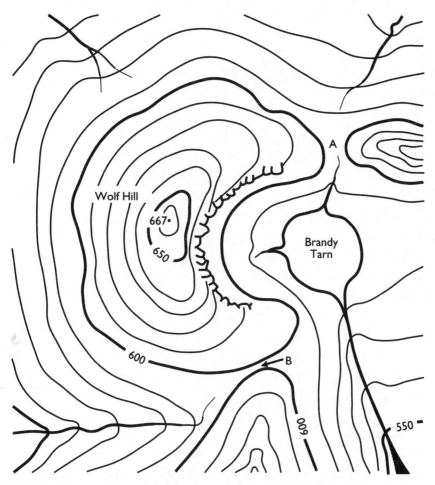

1.4 Thin, or intermediate contours, are sometimes numbered. Index contours, the darker ones, are usually marked with the altitude. Cliffs are marked as shown and sometimes obscure the contour lines. A and B show passes through the ridge.

Every fifth contour is an index contour. Index contours have the height they represent written on them at intervals along their length. Heights always refer to heights above mean sea-level (the level of the sea averaged over many years and many tidal cycles). To determine which way the ground is sloping at a particular place, locate the two nearest index contours and trace them along until you come to their altitudes. Once you know which way the ground is sloping, you can tell whether the 'U's or 'V's you are looking at represent a ridge or a valley.

Very often you will see the tips of the 'U's of two ridges pointing to each other. There are two examples in figure 1.4. This configuration of contour lines represents a pass or saddle. It makes sense; if you started high on either ridge and walked downhill, in the direction the contour 'U's were pointing, you would end up at the pass.

The difference in height between intermediate contours – the *vertical interval* – is always the same on any particular map. Ordnance Survey 1:50 000 and 1:25 000 maps have 10m (33ft) vertical intervals. Likewise, the altitude difference between index contours is also constant. It is always equal to five times the vertical interval, assuming that your map-maker, like most, made every fifth contour line an index contour.

Whatever the vertical interval, the third relief-map principle still applies: the more closely the contours are spaced, the steeper the slope. That is because the denser the contours, the greater the height change over the same horizontal distance. A vertical cliff is the most extreme example: a large height change over zero horizontal distance. Map-makers depict cliffs by drawing contour lines that merge, as illustrated in figure 1.4.

What scale?

In Britain, the Ordnance Survey is the prime source of maps. Most useful for walkers and climbers is the 1:50 000 scale Landranger Series of 204 sheets, each covering an area of 40 x 40km (25 x 25 miles). For more detailed information, including mountain walls, fences and fire-breaks in forest plantations, use the 1:25 000 Pathfinder Series, but remember that it only covers a quarter of the area of the Landranger Series for the same size of map. For popular recreation areas, the Ordnance Survey have specially designed Outdoor Leisure maps using the 1:25 000 scale.

While we are on the matter of scale, let us get one other bit of terminology straight: *small scale* versus *large scale*. On a small-scale map, landscape features are shown relatively small. On a 1:250 000-scale map (Routemaster Series, for example, which uses a relatively small scale) a moor 1km long is only 4mm on the map (or 1 mile is $^1/_4$in on the map), so this scale is of more use to motorists than walkers. On a large-scale map, such as a 1:25 000 Pathfinder, that same 1km of moorland would occupy 4cm (or 1 mile would be $2^1/_2$ in).

All these maps use metric units, and all are criss-crossed with grids of numbered lines − vertical eastings and horizontal northings. We will say more in a later chapter about how to use grid references to state a location very accurately. The grids are also really useful for checking distances. On the Pathfinder and Landranger maps the sides of each grid square represent 1km (0.6 miles) on the ground. The 4-cm ($1^1/_2$-in) grids on the smaller scale Routemaster Series represent distances of 10km (6.2 miles). Although a large-scale map may be used for details of an expedition, a smaller scale map covering a far greater area can be useful for identifying distant peaks in clear weather.

Existing maps are not sufficient on their own for climbing the really jagged peaks of the Black Cuillin in Skye, and should be used together with climbing or scrambling guidebooks. The rocks of the Skye Cuillin and the Rum Cuillin are gabbro intruded with basalt. These mountains are magnetic and affect compasses, so check and recheck your bearings often when moving along the ridges in mist.

It is not important to memorize what 1cm or 1in means in all these different scales. All the maps have a visual reminder at the bottom in the form of a scale showing what distance on the map equals 1km (0.6 miles) on the land. Before studying a map, check the scale, as it will help you to visualize the terrain.

Map colouring is important, but do your planning in good lighting conditions. You may get a shock reading your map inside a green tent when bright sunshine is glaring on snowfields outside. The contour lines virtually disappear and, instead of familiar mountains, you are faced with empty spaces – disconcerting! Also remember that about 10 per cent of males have some form of colour vision problem. Contour lines are printed in red. Mountain areas (Glencoe for example) owned by the National Trust for Scotland are bordered with a red unbroken line, with NTS in red or blue. National Parks and Forest Parks are bordered with broad yellow highlights.

Check the symbols list printed on each map for the reds, oranges and yellows of trunk roads, main roads and minor roads. Blue, logically, denotes water: streams, rivers, lakes, the sea. Also printed in blue on the 1:25 000 Outdoor Leisure and 1:50 000 sheets are surveyors' triangulation pillars (trig. points), National Grid squares, parking places, information centres, viewpoints, camp and picnic sites, etc. The names of Long Distance Paths (for example, the West Highland Way) may be accented in a blue or green strip, or marked LDP. A deeper blue is now used for motorways. Woods and forestry plantations are green.

The Ordnance Survey uses several dozen symbols on its maps to indicate everything from surveyors' trig. points to railways. Figure 1.5 shows some of them. Each Ordnance Survey map shows the road classification symbols.

An illustrated brochure of maps is available free on request from Information and Enquiries, Ordnance Survey, Romsey Road, Maybush, Southampton, SO9 4DH. You can also buy maps from stationers and outdoor shops, the latter of which stock compasses and probably altimeters.

Contour maps depict unchanging physical features very accurately, but as time passes (compilation and revision dates are printed on the map) some natural features are likely to evolve. A

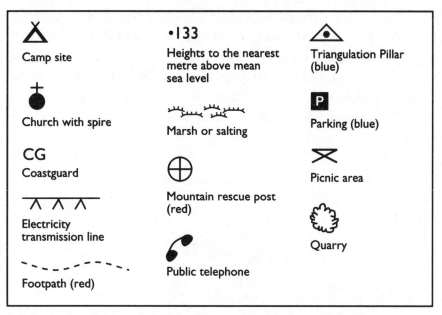

1.5 A selection of map symbols. Fuller lists are printed at the margins of the maps.

lake, for example, may become a meadow; tarns and lochans may change to bog or heathland; trees may grow up to form woodland. Man-made features are very likely to change. Roads will be upgraded and re-routed, or they may be abandoned if a new hydro-dam is built creating a new loch (Loch Loyne above Glen Moriston, for example). Coniferous forests will be planted and felled. New four-wheel-drive roads will appear on the hillsides, or even crossing the high plateaux (for example the Feshie Hills and Beinn a'Bhuird). If you are visiting a National Park or Forest Park, you may be able to keep up with changes by obtaining an up-to-date map from the administration. A friendly ranger might also help you update your map.

Maps are named from some prominent feature or town within their boundaries, for example, 'Ben Nevis' or 'Aberdeen'. Indexes show towns and estuaries, which may help you identify which maps you need. When in doubt about a map, order it anyway. Even if your intended route doesn't cross it, you will probably be looking out at those peaks and valleys when you stop for lunch on the summit.

If you have a map that covers part of the area you are interested in, look at the marginal diagram which will tell you the names of all adjoining maps, including those that only touch at one corner. Outdoor Leisure maps cover special areas. Ordering one of them instead of four or five individual sheets can save you a lot of paperwork when you are out in the field.

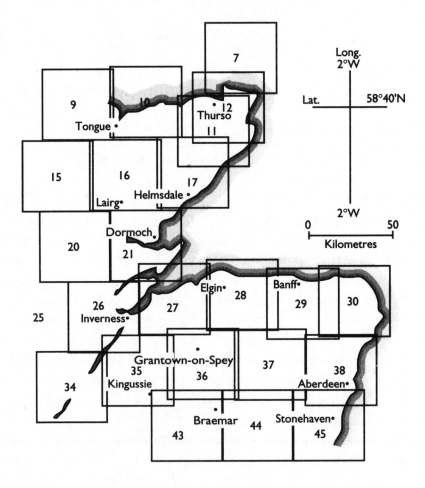

1.6 Sheet numbers of 1:50 000 Ordnance Survey maps covering north-east Scotland. A total of 204 sheets covers Britain.

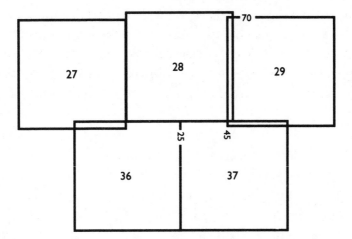

1.7 This diagram is printed in the margin of sheet 28 to show adjoining sheets. The smaller figures give the grid values of the adjoining sheet edges.

How far, how fast?

Maps can tell you two things you really want to know before you launch yourself into the mountains. Can I get there from here? And, how long will it take?

If a path leads to your destination, then all you need to know is the time required. First, calculate the horizontal distance. A ruler makes it easy to measure the straight-line distance, but tracks never run straight. In fact, they are notorious for taking a lot more kilometres to reach a destination than the straight-line distance would indicate.

To calculate distance along a path, use a bit of string or soft wire. Place one end on your starting point, then trace the path with the string, following it as it twists and turns. Use your thumbnail to mark the point where the string crosses your destination, then bring it down to the scale at the bottom of the map and read off the distance. It is a good idea to add a pessimism factor of 10 per cent to account for the curves you shortcut and the switchbacks the map-maker neglected to show.

As an alternative measuring tool, use the edge of your compass. One edge on many models is marked in inches and another in centimetres. Use short, straight distances to approximate curves. As a third option, buy a map-measuring device. The most common ones have a wheel which you roll along the map surface. A pointer indicates kilometres or miles for several different map scales.

Measuring distances by any method is easiest on a flat surface, such as your kitchen table the evening before a day walk, or your tent floor before you strike camp.

After determining the mileage, calculate the height change. First, determine your starting altitude. Find the index contour closest to your starting point, yet still below it, and trace along it until you find a place where the map gives its altitude. Then count the number of intermediate contours between the index contour and your starting point. Multiply the number of intermediate contours by the vertical interval (it is given at the bottom of the map) and add that number to the altitude of the index contour. For example, let us say the closest index contour below your starting point is 300m. The contour interval is 10m, and the road is three contours above the 300-m index contour, so you are at 330m.

Determine the altitude of your destination in the same way. Subtract, and you have your height gain or loss.

In some cases, you may find that the map doesn't give an altitude for the first index contour below your starting point. In that case, find the nearest one which does have an altitude indicated and calculate the altitude of the index contour you need. If every fifth contour is an index contour, as is usual, then the height difference between index contours equals five times the vertical interval. For example, if the contour interval is 10m and every fifth contour is an index contour, the height difference between index contours is 50m.

If the path runs up and down more than once, be sure to add up all the individual segments of height gain.

Now you have the most important information for estimating

travel time: distance and height gain. But there are other variables as well: your fitness, your load, the roughness of the ground, the depth of snow (if any), your mode of transport (foot or skis), and whether you are out for the exercise or to admire wildlife. Three kilometres an hour (2 mph) is a reasonable pace on a level track with a moderate load. For every 600m (2000ft) of height gain, add an hour to the time you calculated for the distance alone. That will give you a very rough estimate. Then go out and walk and ski some tracks. Write down your times over different kinds of terrain, and make sure you add in rest stops. You will soon learn what is reasonable for you.

If no path leads to your destination, getting there may be problematical. Your map can give you important clues to the easiest route, but only an actual visit or a phone call to a knowledgeable local will tell you if your planned route is feasible. Those green areas, for example, may be open woods allowing pleasant strolling, but they may also be nearly impenetrable plantations of conifers. The most important information the map gives to those planning a cross-country journey is probably the average slope of the steepest part of the route.

Find your route's steepest part by locating the place where the contours are closest together. Then measure that horizontal distance. Next, measure the vertical rise over that same horizontal distance.

If the vertical rise is the same as the horizontal distance, you are looking at a 45-degree slope that is likely to be very tough walking. In fact, it probably involves stiff scrambling, and it may confront you with some real cliffs. If the vertical rise is greater than the horizontal distance, you are most likely confronting mountaineering territory where you would be advised to have a rope, some hardware and some well-honed climbing skills.

When the rise is only half the horizontal distance, you are looking at a slope of 27 degrees – steep walking, but that is all. You can probably find your way around any small crags that may be hiding in between the contour lines.

Like all generalizations, these have exceptions. The average angle of the slope climbing out of a ravine may be quite moderate, but the steepest angle is often vertical. Short but impassable cliffs can run for miles without a navigable break.

An example of a 45-degree slope is the East Face of the Devil's Point (1004m/3290ft) not far from Corrour Bothy near the River Dee, Cairngorms. In 400m (1300ft) of horizontal distance the slope rises from 600m to 1000m (2000ft to 3280ft) – a 400m (13000ft) vertical rise – and so is exactly 45 degrees. Any who have crossed the Lairig Ghru and seen this face in profile behind the bothy would not consider it a mere walking route, because it is a slabby face rather than a jagged face. It looks really evil. It all depends on the rock, but this one is definitely a rock-climb.

A slope of about 30 degrees forms the top part of the north-east ridge of the Angel's Peak nearby. It rises from 950m to 1258m (3117ft to 4127ft) in 500m (1640ft) of horizontal distance – not to be undertaken lightly but a reasonable scramble in dry, summer weather. Once again, local experience is the real key.

How long will a cross-country route take you? If you are bashing through deep heather, or bracken amongst boulders, or scrambling amidst cliff bands, the time required is anyone's guess. It could take two hours to travel 1km (0.6 miles). On the other hand, if you are strolling along a smooth, level ridge above the tree line, 1km might take you only 15 minutes. Travelling on skis off-piste can be even slower than travelling cross-country in the summer because of the extra effort of making a track through deep snow. In the summer, if you are fit, carrying only a daypack and moving hard, you may be able to gain 600m (2000ft) in an hour, at least for a while. In most cases, you are likely to do less. If your route combines track- and ridge-walking, you will usually save time if you stick to the track until you are at the pass between two peaks, then follow the line of the ridge to gain your desired summit. Leaving the track when you first catch sight of the peak you want to climb and heading diagonally up a steep slope usually takes longer. As with path-walking, you have to spend some time in the country to learn how map features translate into terrain, and what your personal capabilities are.

It is as well to read a glossary of place names, usually available from the map-makers, to understand terms describing mountain features of the country you are operating in. A pass or col (French) might be 'lairig' or 'bealach' in Highland Gaelic; 'nant' or 'bwlch' in Eryri (Snowdonia); 'hause' or 'nick' in England. A similar saddle in Yorkshire might be described by dalesmen as 't' gap beyond top o't' fell, like'.

2

Choosing and using a compass

A vicious squall raked the treeless tundra below Alaska's Mount Sanford. Snow driven by a 64kph (40mph) gale blew horizontally past the cabin windows. The 7-mm ($^1/_4$-in) thick guy wires supporting the cabin whistled and shrieked as the wind dealt body-blows to the flimsy plywood walls. Visibility – between the gusts – sometimes reached 45m (50yd). Somewhere out in the maelstrom, Chris Haaland and Sara Ballantyne were carrying a load of mountaineering gear toward the foot of Sanford's Sheep Glacier.

Only rolling brown hills dissected by wandering streams lay between the cabin and the glacier. All looked identical, particularly when viewed through ice-encrusted lashes and a punishing veil of flying snow. To make the route-finding even more difficult, Chris and Sara planned to return to the cabin that night, after caching their equipment.

But Chris and Sara had one thing going for them. They knew approximately where the cabin was on the map, and where they wanted to go. Based on that knowledge, they had taken a *course* off the map. In other words, they used a compass to measure the *angle* between true north and the direction they wanted to go.

As soon as they stepped from the cabin, they sighted along their course as far as they could see, picked a landmark and headed in that direction. Whenever they reached a high point – a ridge or hilltop – they built a small pile of stones, a cairn, to aid their return. Cairns should be used only when absolutely necessary, and should be knocked down and scattered during your return trip so that no evidence remains of your passage. Then they sighted along their course again, picked another landmark, and continued.

Eventually they felt rather than saw that they had reached a low pass. Below them lay the Sheep Glacier. They cached their loads, turned around, and began following their cairns towards home. Without the cairns to correct their course periodically in the rough terrain, they might well have wandered away from their route without realizing it. At dusk, with the storm still pounding the tundra outside, they walked into the welcome shelter of the cabin.

Chris and Sara had navigated across 10.5km (6½ miles) of tundra – and back – using nothing but a compass, a few piles of rocks and an initial course taken off the map. Once the storm closed in, the map was of little further use. If they had had even a few minutes visibility before the squalls blew in – just long enough to take a compass bearing off their destination – they wouldn't even have needed the map. Ingenuity and a compass are often enough by themselves to find your way.

The most basic compass is simply a magnetic needle suspended on a pivot so the needle can align itself with the earth's magnetic field. The needle is usually mounted in some kind of circular housing marked with the cardinal directions: north, south, east and west. Although even the simplest compass lets you determine directions roughly, you need something more sophisticated for precise navigation.

First, you need a compass that lets you sight some landmark in the field and take its *bearing*. A bearing is nothing more than the angle between a line heading north from your position and a line heading towards the landmark. The north line can be defined as *true north* (the direction of the North Pole) or *magnetic north* (the direction the compass needle points). For now, study figure 2.1 overleaf and memorize this concept: a bearing is an *angle*, measured in degrees, between a line heading north and a line heading towards your landmark. You always start counting at the north line, and you always count *clockwise* around the compass dial.

Second, you need a compass that lets you measure angles on a map. Once again, the angle of interest will be between a line running north, and a line running through your position and some

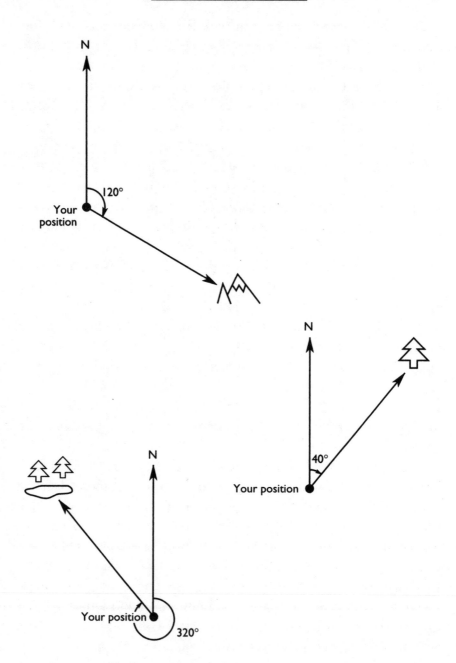

2.1 Bearings are angles, measured clockwise from north. North can be defined as true north or magnetic north.

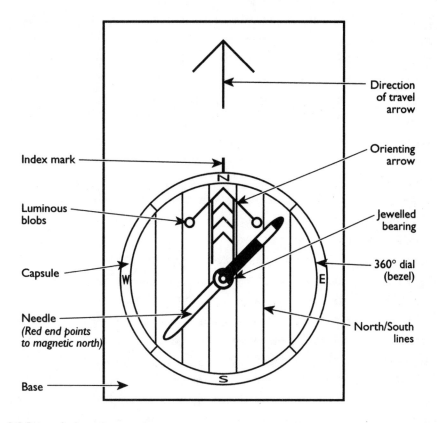

2.2 Parts of a baseplate compass.

mapped landmark. Let us call that angle a *course*, since you will normally use that angle to pick the course you will travel. For that purpose, the compass needle is unnecessary. What you really want is a *protractor*: a device for measuring angles.

Since it is awkward to carry around both a compass and a protractor, compass manufacturers have combined the two instruments in one. They are called *protractor compasses*, or, more commonly, *baseplate compasses*, and they are fundamental to most of the navigational techniques discussed in this book. Figure 2.2 shows their basic parts.

The baseplate compass has a clear rectangular base, with the circular housing for the compass needle mounted at one end. That circular housing, or *capsule*, rotates in relation to the baseplate.

The outer edge is marked north, south, east and west and also marked in degrees, increasing as you move around the capsule clockwise. The markings are sometimes called the *bezel*. Zero degrees equals north; 90 degrees equals east; 180 degrees equals south; 270 degrees equals west and 360 degrees once again equals north, or zero. Inside the capsule, you will usually see a series of parallel lines. They are called north/south lines, because they lie parallel to a line running through the north and south points on the capsule.

Most baseplate compasses have an arrow inscribed on the base. This is called the *direction-of-travel* arrow because it indicates the direction you want to go when the capsule is set to a course you have taken off the map. You point the same arrow at a landmark in the field when you want to measure a bearing. In line with the direction-of-travel arrow is the *index mark*, where you read off the number of degrees to which the capsule is set. To set the capsule to any angle between zero and 360 degrees, turn the capsule until the correct number of degrees is aligned with the index mark.

The compass needle rotates within the capsule, coming to rest when the north end of the needle, usually red, points to magnetic north. Many map and compass operations require you to twist the capsule until the north end of the needle points to the north mark on the capsule. To make it easy to determine when the needle and the capsule's north mark are accurately aligned, the capsule has an orienting arrow inscribed, usually in red, on its bottom surface. The orienting arrow is sometimes called the *gate*, especially in America where it takes the form of a gate, or *coffin*, which is where you may end up if you get it wrong. For brevity we will call it the gate, and if we tell you to 'place the needle in the gate', we mean you to align the orienting arrow with the north-seeking end of the needle, and line up red with red. You may be lucky enough to have a compass with luminous blobs on the orienting arrow barbs and on the red arm of the needle, to make the lining up easier at night.

Together, these three moving parts – baseplate, capsule and

needle – let you measure the bearing of a landmark in the field and measure courses on the map. We will tell you how to do this after we finish discussing compasses.

Some baseplate compasses have a mirror attached to the baseplate with a hinge. When you take a bearing, the mirror lets you see both the object you are sighting and the capsule at the same time. That increases the accuracy of your bearing measurement. The mirror also lets you admire your handsomely weatherbeaten features after a week on expedition – greasy hair, burnt cheeks and all! For the first reason only, we recommend a mirror model.

As we have already mentioned, compass needles almost never point to true north. The difference in direction between true north and magnetic north is an angle called the *variation*. For practical purposes, variation is the difference in direction between *grid* north and magnetic north, except in America, where the angle between true north and magnetic north is called the *declination*. In Britain, Ordnance Survey maps have sketches in the margins showing true, grid and magnetic north (diagrammatic only). From information in the margin you will be able to calculate the difference between grid north and magnetic north – the variation – for that particular map in its year of publication. The grids mentioned in Chapter 1 only line up with true north on the 2 degrees west meridian. In the Outer Hebrides, grid north can be almost 5 degrees off true north because the curved surface of the earth cannot be shown on a flat map.

Compensating for the difference between magnetic and grid north when doing map and compass work with a standard baseplate compass requires some simple addition or subtraction. When you take a bearing in the field, you have measured an angle between magnetic north, indicated by the compass needle, and your landmark. When you take a course off a map, however, you have measured an angle between *grid* north, indicated by the top of the map, and your landmark. You have to reconcile the two means of measurement, a process we will describe later.

If you would rather not mess around with that, you can buy a compass which lets you set the variation and forget it. On standard baseplate compasses, the gate is fixed in relation to the capsule. When you place the north end of the needle in the north part of the gate, the needle points exactly at the north mark on the capsule.

'Set-and-forget' compasses, on the other hand, have a gate that moves in relation to the north mark on the capsule. You set it at an angle to grid north equal to the variation and forget about it until you travel to some different region, where the variation is different. Now, when you place the needle in the gate, the needle points to magnetic north and the north mark on the capsule points to grid north (see figure 2.3). There is no need to do any addition or subtraction, or even to remember what the variation is. Set-and-forget compasses are indeed easier to use. We recommend them.

Every compass worth buying will be fluid-damped, where fluid within the capsule prevents the needle from swinging to and fro like a hypnotist's watch. A good compass will still function at −40°C (−40°F), although it is best to keep it inside your anorak to prevent bubbles from forming as the liquid contracts. High altitude, particularly when combined with severe cold, can also cause a bubble to appear. The bubble will not interfere with accuracy unless it is bigger than 5mm (¼in) in diameter. Usually the bubble will disappear when you return to normal temperatures and sea-level. If it doesn't, you may have a leak. Avoid buying a compass that already has a bubble in the capsule.

You should also protect your compass from extreme heat, such as the dashboard of your car. High temperatures cause the liquid to expand, which can rupture the capsule.

Be sure to buy your compass in the region where you intend to use it. Only along a line known as the *magnetic equator*, which lies near the geographical equator, do compass needles sit level with the earth's surface. North of the magnetic equator, they dip to the north; south of the magnetic equator, they dip to the south. Manufacturers compensate by counter-balancing the compass needle so that the needle pivots freely when the compass is held

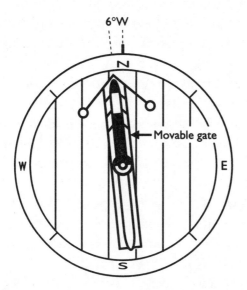

2.3 A set-and-forget compass set for a variation of 6 degrees west. The needle points to magnetic north; the north mark on the capsule indicates grid north.

horizontally. If you take a compass balanced correctly for Britain to Australia, the needle is likely to bind. However, some of the latest compasses have balancing systems which allow you to use them anywhere in the world.

If you buy a mirror-sight compass, be sure the design lets you see the capsule while you sight landmarks both above and below your elevation. You can check in the shop just by sighting something on the floor a couple of metres in front of you, then sighting something on the ceiling, and making sure you can see the capsule and needle while you are sighting.

You can buy compasses with any number of different scales marked along their edges. While those scales can be handy if they happen to match the scale of the map you are using, they are not a sufficient reason to buy a particular compass. After all, you can always copy the scale from the map you will be using on your next trip and tape it to your compass.

It will make our job – and yours – a lot easier if you go out and buy yourself a baseplate compass and contour map before you continue reading this book. There is nothing like having the real thing in your hands to make all this talk of aligning needles in gates and twisting capsules to different bearings seem as simple as it really is. If a picture is worth a thousand words, then actual experience is worth ten thousand.

Now you have a map and compass in your hands, you are about ready to use them. But first you need to know about a common pitfall. John Hinde tells a story that illustrates the point perfectly.

'One day, several years ago in Cyprus, I was assessing half a dozen candidates for their Mountain Leadership Certificates. When we were close to a huge boulder I asked them all to take the magnetic bearing of a peak about 2km (1 mile) distant. Normally the readings would vary by 2 or 3 degrees, and it would be wise to use the average value. Their readings differed widely by about 10 or 15 degrees, and none of them could think of the explanation. The rock was magnetic, of course, and compasses held right against the boulder had wildly swinging needles. Standing up and walking a few paces away from the rock freed the needle from its influence. The moral is to use your compass warily in that type of country, taking averages of several readings.'

Strong magnetic anomalies are fortunately rare in Britain, but do not use your compass resting on an iron fence post, on the roof of the car, or in the same hand as your ice-axe. Any metal object, even much smaller ones such as pocket knives and belt buckles, can throw off the compass needle. The same is true of all electronic devices. Whenever current flows through a wire, it generates a magnetic field which can affect the compass needle.

Before using your compass, therefore, make sure that nothing metallic or electronic is affecting it. Once you have done that, trust it.

Taking a bearing

The first technique to learn is how to take a bearing off a land-mark, then walk that bearing. Since you are not, at this time, relating your bearings to a map, there is no need to worry about the difference between true north, or grid north, and magnetic north. You can simply relate all directions to magnetic north.

Let us assume you bought a baseplate compass without a mirror sight. To take a bearing off a landmark in the field, point the direction-of-travel arrow at the landmark. Hold the compass level, so the needle can swing freely. Now hold the baseplate still and rotate the capsule until you have put the needle in the gate – in other words, until the north end of the needle points to the north mark on the capsule. Then read the bearing at the index mark.

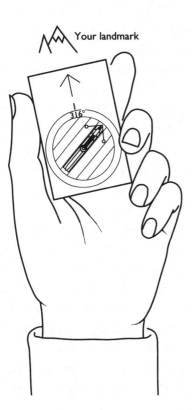

Your landmark

2.4 To take a bearing on a landmark, point the direction-of-travel arrow at the landmark and place the north end of the needle in the north end of the gate. Read the bearing at the index mark.

Figure 2.4 on the previous page shows you how. In this example, the bearing is 316 degrees.

All that you have done is to measure the angle between a line heading towards magnetic north, as indicated by the compass needle, and a line heading towards your landmark, as indicated by the direction-of-travel arrow. The angle is always measured clockwise around the compass dial, starting at north.

Taking a bearing with a mirror-sight compass is essentially the same. The only difference is that the mirror-sight compass allows you to sight on your landmark more accurately.

You can use a mirror-sight compass just like an ordinary baseplate compass. To do so, open the mirror housing all the way, until the compass lies flat. On most models, a line will be inscribed on the mirror. It lies parallel to the long edges of the compass, and starts at a notch in the centre of the cover's top edge. That line serves as the direction-of-travel arrow. Then proceed as you would with a standard compass.

For more accuracy, however, hold the compass level at about the height of your chin. You will have to adjust the height a bit if you are sighting an object either above or below your position. Now open the mirror cover until you can see the capsule in the mirror. Hold the compass so that the line inscribed on the mirror passes directly through the needle's pivot point as you look at the reflection of the capsule. Doing that ensures that the long edges of the compass point directly at the landmark. Now sight the landmark through the notch in the centre of the cover's top edge. Place the needle in the gate by twisting the capsule. Double-check that the line on the mirror is still passing through the needle's pivot point, and read the bearing at the index mark.

Now you have a bearing on your landmark. Let us say that you, like Chris and Sara, want to walk towards this particular landmark. Just after you start, a storm rolls in, so you are forced to navigate by compass. Or perhaps you have climbed to a hill-top and want to take a different way down. You can see your destination – a lake, let us say – but, shortly after you drop off the summit, you will be in thick woods and the lake will be invisible. You could just start out walking the bearing, estimating you will get there in an hour or two. But walking in a straight line in rough terrain is a lot tougher than you would expect. Once you have a bearing on your distant landmark, sight through the compass again, but this time, pick a landmark close at hand. In really foul weather or in the woods that might mean something only a hundred metres away. Walk to that object, sight again, and pick another landmark at the limit of good visibility. Continue until you reach your destination.

Suppose you encounter some obstacle you cannot walk over as you follow your compass bearing. It could be a lake; it could be a stream where you will have to walk up or down to find a ford or fallen log; it could be a wide crevasse in a glacier or a hill ringed with cliffs. If you can see across the obstacle, the solution is simple. Sight along your bearing to some object on the far side of the obstacle, do whatever you have to do to get around it, and walk to the object you sighted. Pick another landmark along your former line of travel, and continue.

If you cannot see across the obstacle – because the fog is too thick, or you are facing a cliff – then you will have to maintain your sense of direction while you skirt round it. First, decide if you want to go around the obstacle to the right or left. Let us say right looks easier. Make a right-angle (90-degree) turn to your right and walk far enough to clear the obstacle. Count double paces as you go, this is much easier than counting single steps. Now turn 90 degrees to your left, which puts you back on your original bearing, and walk until you are sure you have cleared the obstacle. There is no need to count paces here. Make another left-hand 90-degree turn and walk the same number of double paces you counted after your first turn. That puts you back on your original line of travel. Turn right, sight a landmark on your original bearing, and proceed. All you have done is walk three sides of a rectangle so that, when you arrive on the far side of the obstacle,

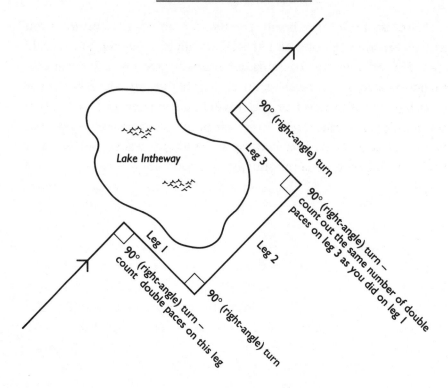

2.5 Maintaining your course while circumventing an obstacle.

you are back on your original line of travel. Figure 2.5 makes all this clear.

To simplify making all those 90-degree turns, use the short edges of the baseplate to sight landmarks. To make the initial 90-degree right turn, for example, face in roughly the correct direction and sight along a short edge of the baseplate while keeping the needle in the gate. Pick a landmark and go, counting your double paces. When you have cleared the obstacle, make the first left turn by sighting an object along your original bearing, using the compass in the normal way. To make the second left turn, face in roughly the correct direction and sight again along a short edge of the baseplate with the needle in the gate. Pick a landmark, pace out your measured distance and you are back on track.

42

To return home, you want to walk in exactly the opposite direction – 180 degrees opposite. To do so, you can either add or subtract 180 degrees to or from your original bearing. Use what ever operation keeps the result between zero and 360 degrees. Or you can align the south end of the needle in the north end of the gate on the capsule. Either operation will point you towards home. You then pick landmarks and walk towards them in exactly the same way you did when heading out.

3

Using compass and map together

The call was urgent: a party of men, young and fit, but inexperienced and with unsuitable boots, had tried to climb Ben Nevis from the south-east, up Coire Giubhsachan. One had slipped on hard snow and fallen a long way with serious injuries. Two others had slipped going to help him, and had both been killed by long falls. John Hinde relates the story:

'I was running a winter skills course for the Royal Air Force mountain rescue teams. There were plenty of trained people to cope with the emergency down in Glen Nevis, but when I first heard it was late in the day and I did not know the two would-be-rescuers had died. I decided that I was needed as I assumed the teams had three serious casualties to deal with at one time. I was staying at the Charles Inglis Clark Memorial Hut, half way up Ben Nevis but under the great cliffs on the other side of the mountain from the accident. I knew that my companion, Dougal Haston, would also be very useful. One of the most active Scottish climbers of that time, I had hired him to take the lads up a few routes. He was reluctant, thinking we were off on a wild-goose chase, but I dragged him away from the warm stove and comfortable bunks.

'Although only 2km (just over a mile) away from the accident site, we had to climb 400m (1300ft), over the Carn Mór Dearg Arête before going down to the calamity. In half darkness we walked up the Allt a'Mhuilinn, fully geared up, to the toe of the North East Buttress. We were heading into the clouds, but neither of us bothered to check our compasses. We knew precisely where we were going; both Dougal and I had been there many times. Possibly each of us thought the other was navigating. The weather was not bad but it was almost dark and very cloudy. All we had to do was to head south into Upper Coire Leis, over a snow-covered boulder field, keeping the steep crags of the Little Brenva Face on our right.

'Not only had we not confirmed we were still heading south, we also failed to note the timing. We were both so sure of ourselves, moving fairly fast, chatting away. Where else could we be going except where we imagined? We were doing a rising diagonal traverse with steep ground to our right. Even when we began to wonder when the ground would steepen into the snow slope or broken rocks with an easy route to the arête, we still did not check our compasses. If we had we would have found we were heading almost north, not south. We had described a semicircle on the map, a rising hairpin leftwards around the head of the Allt a'Mhuilinn. We had not climbed steeply enough, and we had not gone south. Anything but; we had gone east and then north instead!

'Our moment of truth came when the cloud suddenly lifted and we saw the lights of Corpach on Loch Linnhe below us. We were high on the 35-degree slope of Carn Dearg Meadhonach, almost directly above our starting point, the CIC Hut.

'Just as we headed out of the clouds, we also moved into radio intervisibility, and a signal came through. The rescue and recoveries were over; our friends had done the job without us. I decided not to inform the radio linkman of our exact location. I can't remember if Dougal or I confessed afterwards. This may be the first time the cat (or wild goose) has been let out of the bag!

'As we demonstrated, the best map and compass skills in the world are worthless if you don't pull out the tools and use them. It can be really hard to locate your position if the first time you check your map is long after you have wandered

COLEG POWYS - BRECON

away from the last landmark you could identify. It is particularly hard to find yourself if you don't keep track of the direction you are travelling. That sounds obvious, but as we showed, anyone can get cocky about their ability to navigate without navigational tools.'

Orienting the map

The best place for your first map check is the top of the road. First, find your location on the map. Usually this is easy: you are at the end of the road, or at the marked point where the path leaves it. Sometimes, it is not so obvious, such as when you are starting a cross-country walk. If you haven't parked near some obvious, mapped landmark, you may need to use the more sophisticated techniques I describe later to pinpoint your position.

Next, orient the map. In other words, place the map on some flat surface so that directions on the map correspond to directions in the field. It is always easiest to visualize what you are doing if the map is oriented. Sometimes you can orient it by eye. If there is a lake straight ahead of you, and a prominent hill to your right, twist the map until the lake lies straight ahead of your position on the map and the hill is to the right of that position. Here is another way to look at it: a map is oriented correctly if a line drawn on the map from your map position to the mapped lake points straight towards the real lake. In similar fashion, all other directions on the map will also correspond to reality.

Sometimes, you can't orient by eye. The landscape may lack any obvious mapped features, or it may have too many features, and you can't tell which is which. In that case, you need to use your compass to orient the map.

Here, and for the rest of this chapter, we are going to assume that magnetic north and grid north lie in exactly the same direction. That assumption will make it a lot easier for you to learn. In the next chapter we will tell you how to compensate for the difference that usually exists between those directions.

On almost all maps, north is at the top of the sheet. To orient the map roughly, hold the compass horizontal and glance at the needle. It points north, of course. Now twist the map so the top also points north. Note that, when the map is oriented correctly, the left and right margins represent lines running north and south.

To orient the map more accurately, set the capsule to zero degrees. Place the compass on the map so one long edge of the baseplate lies along either the left or right margin. Now rotate map and compass together as a unit until you have placed the needle in the gate, so the north end of the needle points to the north mark on the capsule. The map is now oriented. Every direction on the map corresponds to directions in reality. Figure 3.1 shows a correctly oriented map.

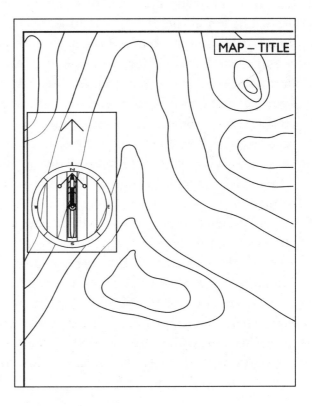

3.1 Orienting the map.

Locating your position

Now that you have found your position and oriented the map, take a look around and identify some nearby landmarks. Determine your general direction-of-travel. Does your route run north, south, east or west? Try to develop a feel for the relationship between the cardinal directions and major terrain features. You might note, for example, that the valley you will be walking up runs east and west, while the region's highest peak is basically to the north. Knowing where you started and in what direction you are travelling will help prevent silly mistakes such as placing the south end of the compass needle in the north end of the gate.

And while you have the map out, try to create a mental image of the terrain you will be travelling through. Maybe you head east up that glen then turn sharp left just past a big cliff, leaving the main track and following a side path that climbs towards a pass to the north. Knowing that kind of thing will help you start looking for a junction at the appropriate time. Don't rely on a sign to jolt you into looking up from your companion's boot heels.

Make a point of getting out your map and compass every hour or so to locate your position on the map. Note the time you started and the time it takes you to reach various landmarks – that path junction, for example. It will give you a sense of your pace that day, which will help you to keep track of your location.

Let us say your goal for the day is the summit of some peak. You reach it at lunchtime and sit down to admire the panorama of mountains spread out before you. Orienting your map will give you a rough idea which peak is which. If you want to know accurately, however, you will need to get a bit more sophisticated.

First, take a bearing on the peak you are interested in, using the technique described in the previous chapter. A glance back at figure 2.4 on page 39 should refresh your memory. That bearing, you will recall, is just the angle between a line heading north and a line leading to the peak. The angle is measured clockwise from the north line. Although you used the direction-of-travel arrow or notch in the mirror to sight the object, note that you would have arrived at exactly the same result if you had sighted along one long edge of the baseplate.

Now you are going to transfer that angle to the map. One line of the angle, represented by the compass gate, will point north; the other line, represented by one long edge of the baseplate, will run right through your position and towards the peak you are interested in.

To make the logic of the next step easier, orient the map before continuing, then reset the compass to the bearing you have just measured. Now place the compass on the map so that the compass gate points north, towards the top of the map, and one long edge of the baseplate sits on top of your position. Note that the long edges of the gate (and the north/south lines in the capsule) run parallel to the right and left margins of the map. Don't twist the capsule in relation to the baseplate. Ignore the compass needle. You are simply using the compass as a protractor now, so the needle is irrelevant.

The long edge of the baseplate that is sitting on top of your position now points directly at the peak you are interested in. Figure 3.2 overleaf shows a compass placed correctly on the map. Note – this is important – that you must make sure you follow the long edge of the baseplate in the direction indicated by the direction-of-travel arrow. With the map oriented correctly, you will see that the long edge of the baseplate not only points to the paper mountain – its also points to the real one.

Often the edge of the baseplate isn't long enough to reach from your location to the peak of interest. You need an extension: a plastic ruler. Not a metal one: you don't want any metal sirens singing to your needle. Place one edge of the ruler alongside the edge of the baseplate that runs through your position. The ruler will now extend towards the peak of interest, making it easy to identify the correct one.

Your map and compass will also help you to solve the opposite puzzle. Once again, let us assume that you know where you are on the map. This time, you want to use the map to tell you which

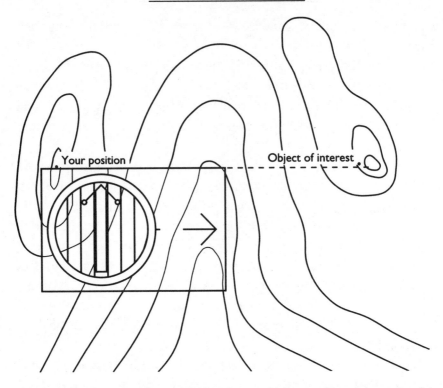

3.2 Applying a bearing taken in the field to the map. Make sure that one long edge of the compass sits on your position, that the north/south lines run north and south and that the north end of the capsule points to the north end of the map. Note that the magnetic needle has been omitted.

way to go. Suppose you are down in the woods at Lake Hereweare and want to know the direction to Lake Overthere.

To solve this problem, you need to measure an angle on the map and transfer it to the terrain. The angle, called a *course*, will be the angle between a line heading north and a line heading to your destination, with your position as the point of the angle.

Start by laying one of the long edges of the baseplate along an imaginary line connecting your position and your destination. Sometimes, as in figure 3.3, the baseplate will be long enough to extend between the two; other times you will need to get out your ruler again to position the baseplate accurately. Be sure the direction-of-travel arrow points at your destination. Now twist the capsule

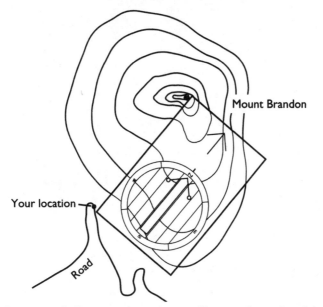

Mount Brandon

Your location

Road

3.3 The first step in finding a course on the map. Place one long edge of the baseplate along an imaginary line connecting your position and your destination. Make sure the direction-of-travel arrow points at your destination

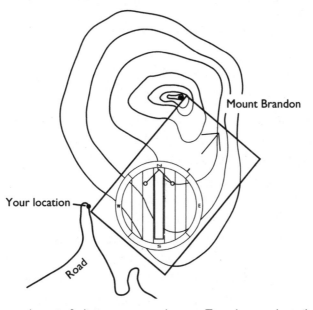

Mount Brandon

Your location

Road

3.4 The second step in finding a course on the map. Turn the capsule until the north/south lines run north and south and the north end of the capsule points north. Note that the magnetic needle has been omitted.

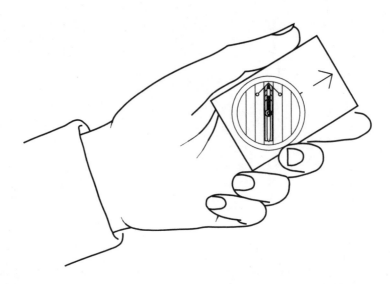

3.5 Using a course measured on a map to determine the direction to your destination in the field. Without moving the capsule in relation to the baseplate, place the needle in the compass gate. The direction-of-travel arrow now points at your destination.

until the gate points north, as shown in figure 3.4 on the previous page. Both the long edges of the gate, and the north/south lines, will run parallel to the left and right margins of the map. Once again, you are using the compass as a protractor, so the needle's gyrations are irrelevant. Read the course – the angle – at the index mark, where the direction-of-travel arrow abuts the compass dial.

To transfer that angle to the field, pick up your compass and rotate it as a unit, without moving the capsule in relation to the baseplate, until you have placed the needle in the gate. As shown in figure 3.5, the direction-of-travel arrow now points in the direction you want to go. Pick a landmark, walk to it, pick another landmark, and proceed.

There is a simple trick that lets you use your ruler to align the

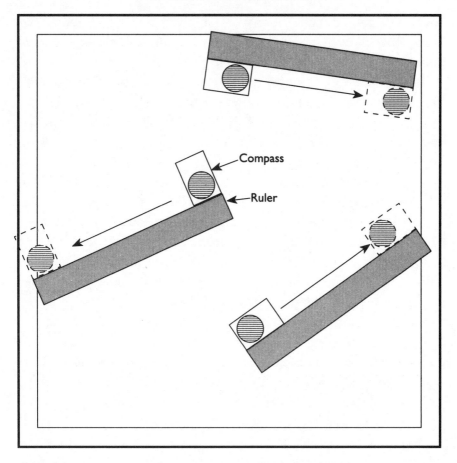

3.6 Using a ruler to align the north/south lines with the edges of the map.

north/south lines more accurately with true north and south. As before, place your compass so that one long edge extends between your position and your destination. Butt your ruler up against that edge in such a way that one end of the ruler touches either the right or left edge of the map. Slide your compass along the ruler until the capsule is set over a margin. Now you can use the margin to align the north/south lines accurately. Figure 3.6 illustrates this technique. The ruler won't always reach the edge of the map, of course, and you need a pretty flat surface to work on. But it is still a useful trick to know when you need high accuracy and conditions permit you to use it. Note that on OS maps the ruler is only needed for identifying distant mountain summits in good visibility. OS maps have all-over grids which make the ruler unnecessary at most times.

Now you are pointing in the right direction: you have a course, taken from the map. But, as Glenn Randall and three friends discovered during the first day of the Colorado Grand Tour, the game is not over. You haven't reached your destination yet.

'It was stormy, with intense winds and near-zero visibility. (You rarely need a map and compass above the tree line when the weather is good. Just pay attention to your surroundings.) My friends were all ex-Outward Bound instructors. I had guided a couple of expeditions on Mount McKinley. We were bound – we hoped – for Vail, 160km (100 miles) and seven days away. But the major storm blasting the Front Range threatened to thwart us only hours after we started. We lunched at a drafty wilderness cabin, then climbed another half a kilometre ($^{1}/_{4}$ mile) to a knoll clearly marked on the map. From there we needed to follow a broad ridge down through a saddle, then up to the Rollins Pass Road. It didn't seem possible to get lost following a ridge. Furthermore, we had all done this leg of the tour before. Just to be sure, Kim Miller dug out the map and compass and determined our course: 270 degrees, due west. We pushed on, leaning into the wind like circus clowns with weighted shoes, heads bowed, our faces so swaddled in face masks and goggles that we felt like astronauts walking on the moon.

'Half an hour slipped away – much longer than it should have taken to reach the steep climb leading up to the road. Kim pulled out his compass and called a halt.

'"Guess what," he said, "we're heading east". We crowded round in disbelief. In the storm, we had walked in a complete semicircle and were facing the way we had come.

'We corrected the course and tried to hurry, but it was still two hours after dark when we arrived in Winter Park, the first night's stop. The moral was clear: when the weather is foul, you not only need to check your compass; you need to check it frequently. Using it correctly once doesn't guarantee safe arrival. Keep your compass in your pocket or around your neck, so you will have no excuse not to use it.'

In the examples above, we assumed you knew your location on the map, but wanted to know the name of a distant peak or the direction in which you should travel. Now let us assume you don't know your location, but you can identify some landmark.

John Hinde and two friends encountered an easy example of that kind of problem on a winter expedition from Corriechoille, Spean Bridge to Lairig Leacach Bothy.

'We knew basically where we were, climbing south-east up the track. But our packs were heavy (we had overnight camping gear as well as ski-mountaineering equipment) and we wanted to know our exact location on the track. (What we really wanted to know was how much longer we would have to suffer beneath those packs.) So I took a bearing on the swell of the summit of Cruach Innse. Once again I had an angle between a line running north and a line leading to a landmark. I knew my position had to be along the line of the angle that passed through the apparent summit. So I placed one long edge of the baseplate on the apparent summit swell and rotated the whole compass, without turning the capsule in relation to the baseplate, until the north/south lines ran north and south, with the direction-of-travel arrow pointing at the landmark. Now I knew I had to be along the line of position defined by that long edge of the baseplate. Since I also knew I was on the track, I had to be at the intersection of my line of position and the track [as shown in figure 3.7 overleaf].

'If the edge of the baseplate hadn't reached from the summit to the trail, I would have needed a ruler or pencil to extend it.'

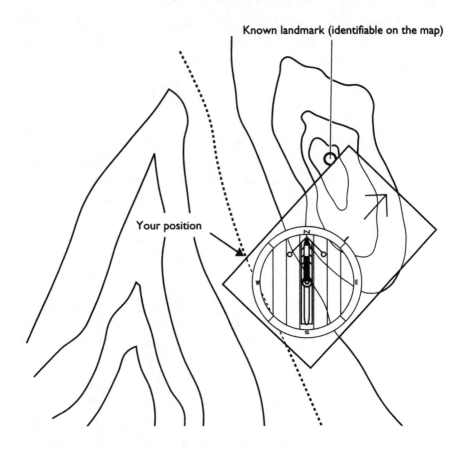

3.7 Determining your position along a track by measuring a bearing to a landmark identifiable on the map.

You don't need to be on a track to use this technique. You could just as well be following a stream, river, pronounced ridge, or the bank of a large lake. Any kind of prominent, linear terrain feature will do. In all cases, the best accuracy comes from picking a landmark at right angles to the terrain feature you are following.

If you can identify two landmarks, you don't even need to be following a terrain feature. Simply take a bearing off one, and pencil in your line of position on the map. Then take a bearing off the second, and pencil in that line of position. Your location is the intersection of the two lines. Figure 3.8 shows you how to do

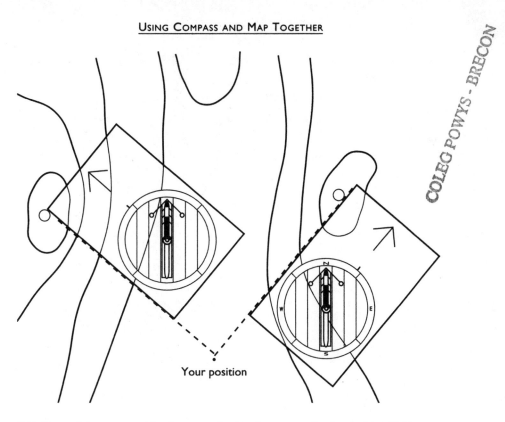

COLEG POWYS - BRECON

3.8 Determining your position by measuring bearings to two landmarks identifiable on the map.

this. If you can take a bearing off a third landmark and pencil in that line of position, so much the better. Your true position should lie somewhere inside the triangle formed by the three lines of position.

Once you have identified your location with lines of position, perform a 'reality check'. If the lines cross at a stream, and you are standing on a ridge, something is wrong. After we identified our position along the trail to the bothy, we took a close look at the map. We had just walked up a rising section of track and gained a nearly level stretch. Our line of position from the summit crossed the track right where the contours became widely spaced – in other words, where the terrain suddenly flattened out. Our location as determined by a line of position checked with the other information we had about the terrain. Whenever you use map and compass together, it is a good idea to perform that kind of reality check on the results, the key to which is being able to visualize terrain from looking at a map. You can learn a certain amount of that from this book, but to really develop that skill, you need to practise out in the field.

4

How to correct for variation

Sometimes reading explanations of how to reconcile grid north and magnetic north is like watching a clown cross his arms, point in opposite directions and say, 'He went that-away'. But fear not, there is a simple, easy to comprehend way to solve variation problems. You just need to remember some straightforward logic. You can forget silly rhymes such as 'grid to mag, add; mag to grid, get rid'. This was once taught by the armed services, but it only works if the variation is west. Just as the forces may have to operate in countries where the variation is opposite, you will probably want to climb outside Britain.

British maps are oriented to the National Grid. If you use maps without the crossed lines of the grid, check in the margin that the map has been printed with its side edges aligned true, or geographic, north and south, and for 'grid north' below read 'true north'.

True north is the direction to the geographic North Pole – one end of the earth's axis of rotation – but in this chapter we shall use grid north. Magnetic north, with reservations explained later, is the direction in which a compass needle points. We are calling *variation* the difference in direction between grid north and magnetic north. Variation, therefore, is an angle, measured with grid north as the starting point. In Britain, magnetic north lies to the west of grid north (to the left, or anti-clockwise, as we look at a map), and we say that the variation is west. West variation is measured anti-clockwise. (This is in contrast to bearings and courses, which are always measured clockwise.) If magnetic north lies 6 degrees west of grid north, the variation is 6 degrees west, not

354 degrees east. Remember that in countries with east variation the variation is measured to the right looking at the map, or clockwise, the same as the bearings.

The beautiful Bradford Washburn map John Hinde used in Alaska in 1962 was printed without grid lines, with the sides aligned true north and south, and with the average variation (mean declination) expressed as 26 degrees north-east. In the east of the United States (Maine) the variation is about 20 degrees west. An *agonic line*, where the compass needle points to true north, runs from the Great Lakes to Florida. In Europe, another agonic line runs through the eastern Mediterranean Sea.

Ignoring the correction for variation can lead you seriously astray, and raise the rude possibility of eating shoe leather for dinner as you bask in the warmth of your cigarette lighter. For each degree that your course is in error and each kilometre (0.6 miles) that you travel, you will be off by about 18m (60ft). If the variation is 6 degrees, you will be off by over 200m (650ft) after walking just 2km (1 mile). It is pretty hard to find your tent if 200m (650ft) of plantation or fog separates you from it.

Strictly speaking, it is incorrect to say 'the compass needle points to the magnetic north pole'. What the needle actually does is align itself with the earth's magnetic field. Compass needles may or may not actually point at the magnetic north pole itself, which, in 1981, lay just north of Bathurst Island in Canada's Northwest Territories. For reasons not well understood, the magnetic poles move slowly, over periods of many years, through circular paths with a diameter of about 160km (100 miles).

But, for a hill-walker, all that doesn't matter. If you are using the most recent OS map available, the variation it gives will be accurate to within a degree or two. Although variation changes slowly as you travel east or west, you can assume that the needle always points in the same direction within the bounds of the area you cover in a typical human-powered trip. In Scotland, for example, you would have to travel between the Isle of Skye and

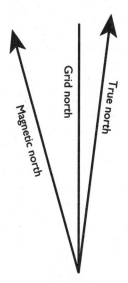

At the centre of this sheet true north is 0°17' east of grid north. Magnetic north is estimated at 5½° west of grid north for 1991, decreasing about ½° in three years.

4.1 Typical marginal notes
(Outdoor Leisure Series)

Typical diagram
(Landranger Series)

Strathdon, east or west about 150km (93 miles) for the variation to change 1 degree. Similarly, from north to south in Britain, say from the Orkneys to Southampton, there is proportionally less change in magnetic variation. For the sake of simplicity, let us just say the compass needle points to magnetic north.

OS Outdoor Leisure maps have bottom margin notes on variation similar to those shown in figure 4.1. Landranger Series maps (1:50 000) have notes on variation, tables of differences of true north from grid north at sheet corners, and variation diagrams in the right margin. True north and magnetic north are arrowed; while grid north is unarrowed.

Let us assume for the moment that you didn't spend the extra money to buy a set-and-forget compass. Before you can understand how to correct for variation with a standard baseplate compass, you need to understand two facts. First, every angle that you measure on a *map* is measured *clockwise*, with *grid north* as the

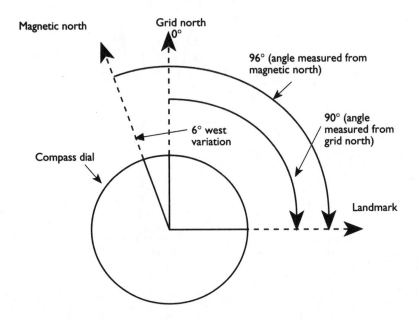

Magnetic north

Grid north
0°

96° (angle measured from magnetic north)

90° (angle measured from grid north)

6° west variation

Compass dial

Landmark

4.2 The relationship between grid north angles and magnetic north angles for a variation of 6 degrees west.

starting point. The needle is irrelevant. You are simply using the compass as a protractor. Second, every angle that you measure in the *field* by placing the needle in the gate of the *compass* is also measured *clockwise*, but the starting point is *magnetic north*.

Let us refer to angles with grid north as the starting point as grid bearings or grid courses. (They are essentially the same. A bearing is just a direction to a landmark; a course is a direction you will follow.) All angles measured with a compass, using magnetic north as the starting point, will be *magnetic north bearings* or *magnetic north courses*.

Now let us assume that you are walking in the Cairngorms, where the variation is always west. Take a look at figure 4.2.

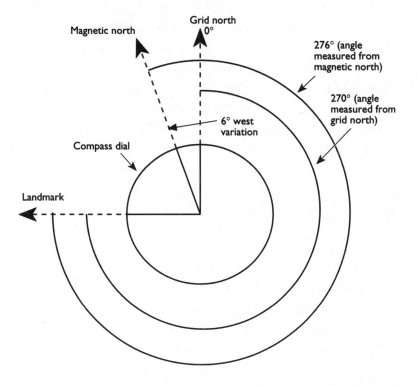

4.3 A second example of the relationship between grid north angles and magnetic north angles for a variation of 6 degrees west.

Grid north is marked zero degrees. Magnetic north is marked 6 degrees. It lies to the west of grid north. In other words, the variation is 6 degrees west. Now let us say you measure a course on the map to a landmark and find it to be 90 degrees. That is a grid north course; you started measuring at grid north, just as the diagram shows. Now if you take a bearing on the landmark with your compass, you will find the bearing to be 96 degrees. That is a magnetic north bearing, since you started measuring at magnetic north.

The grid north angle, measured on the map, is less than the magnetic north angle measured in the field with the compass by placing the needle in the gate. Furthermore, the difference is 6 degrees – exactly the amount of the variation. And that leads to our first conclusion: *when the variation is west, grid north angles (bearings and courses) are always going to be less than magnetic north angles (bearings and courses).* If you measure an angle on the map and want to transfer it to your compass, you must add the variation to the grid north angle because magnetic north angles are always greater than true north angles when the variation is west. If you measure an angle with your compass and want to transfer it to the map, you must subtract the variation, because grid north angles are always less than magnetic north angles when the variation is west.

You don't need to memorize these rules. Just remember the logic behind them. If you need to jog your memory, look at the variation diagram in the margin of the map.

If magnetic north is west (anti-clockwise, or to the left of grid north), then every angle measured clockwise from grid north must be less than the same angle measured clockwise from magnetic north. To reinforce this concept one more time, look at figure 4.3 on the previous page. It shows the relationship between magnetic north and grid north for a situation where the grid north bearing is 270 degrees.

The same logic applies if the declination is east, as it is in the Colorado Rockies (note that, in the United States, variation is known as declination). Look at figure 4.4. The declination is 10 degrees, but this time it is east. Let us say you measure an angle on the map (starting at true north) as 90 degrees. If you measure the same angle in the field with your compass, starting at magnetic north, you will get 80 degrees. The difference, 10 degrees, is equal to the declination. That leads to our second conclusion: *when the declination is east, true north angles (bearings and courses) are always going to be greater than magnetic north angles (bearings and courses).* If you measure an angle on the map and want to transfer it to your compass, you must subtract the declination from the true north angle, because magnetic north angles are always less than true north angles when the declination is east. If you

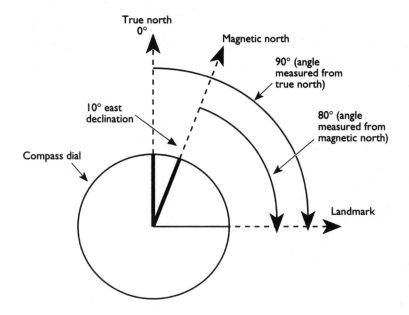

4.4 The relationship between true north angles and magnetic north angles for a declination of 10 degrees east.

measure an angle with your compass and want to transfer it to the map, you must add the declination to the magnetic angle for the same reason: true north angles are always greater than magnetic north angles when the declination is east. Again, the declination diagram in the bottom margin of the map should help to refresh your memory.

Figure 4.5 overleaf gives another example of the relationship between magnetic and true north when the declination is east, this time for a true north angle of 270 degrees.

In Britain, it is possible to measure a grid north angle on the map, then find, when you add the west variation, that you have gone past 360 degrees. For example, you might measure a grid north angle on the map as 358 degrees, then need to add a variation of 6 degrees west to get the magnetic angle: 358+6=364. An

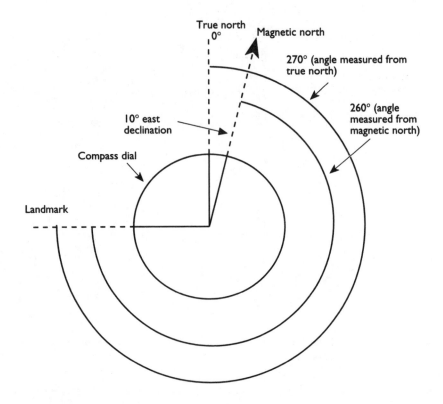

4.5 A second example of the relationship between true north angles and magnetic north angles for a declination of 10 degrees east.

angle of 364 degrees is the same as an angle of 4 degrees. You can also just rotate the compass dial anti-clockwise 6 degrees to add 6 degrees to the grid north angle of 358 degrees and get the correct magnetic north angle of 4 degrees. Figure 4.6 shows this graphically.

In the American West, you may measure a true north angle on the map, find it is less than the declination, then need to subtract the declination from the true north angle to get the magnetic north angle. For example, the true north angle measured on the map might be 5 degrees, and you will have to subtract a declina-

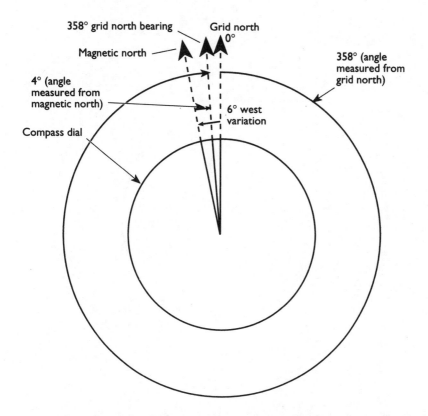

4.6 The relationship between a grid north angle of 358 degrees and a magnetic north angle of 4 degrees when the variation is 6 degrees west.

tion of 10 degrees east. Five degrees is the same as 365 degrees, so you can just subtract 10 from 365 and get 355 degrees as the correct magnetic north angle. You can also just rotate the dial clockwise 10 degrees from its original setting of 5 degrees to do the subtraction and reach the correct magnetic north setting of 355 degrees, as shown in figure 4.7 overleaf.

Some people recommend scribing lines on your maps that run towards magnetic north, then aligning the capsule's north/south lines along those magnetic meridians whenever you measure an angle on the map. That way, your starting point for measuring an

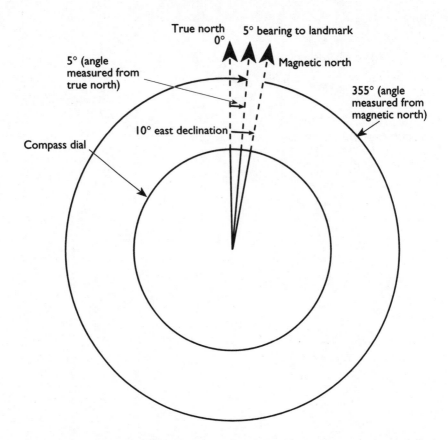

4.7 The relationship between a true north angle of 5 degrees and a magnetic north angle of 355 degrees when the declination is 10 degrees east.

angle is always the same, whether you measure it on the map or measure it with the compass. Scribing lines is fine if you have only a few maps to do, and a drafting table on which to do it accurately. However, it is much easier to remember the logic of adding and subtracting. Since most people do the majority of their walking in one area, they only need to remember one line of logic. In the American West, true north angles are always greater than magnetic north angles; in Britain, grid north angles are always smaller than magnetic north angles.

If you are using a set-and-forget compass, you can forget about adding and subtracting once you have set the variation and double-checked that you set it in the right direction. With most such compasses, setting the variation is idiot-proof. Usually you turn a small screw or perform some other simple operation to adjust the compass gate so that it points to the angle representing the variation. If the variation is 6 degrees west, for example in the Cairngorms, the compass gate (orienting arrow) would point to 354 degrees (360−6 = 354). In Alaska, if the declination is 26 degrees east, for example, the compass gate, after adjustment, would point to 26 degrees.

When you are measuring an angle on the map with a set-and-forget compass, you ignore the needle (as always) and the compass gate (which no longer points to north on the capsule). Instead, you always use the capsule's north/south lines when orienting the capsule north and south, making sure north on the capsule points to north on the map. To transfer that angle to your compass, simply place the needle in the gate. Angles measured with your compass can be transferred directly to the map, again using the north/south lines in the capsule, not the gate. As you can see, set-and-forget compasses let you avoid mental gymnastics when you are cold, wet and would much rather think about dinner courses than compass courses. They also let you avoid spending lots of time drawing lines on your maps. In the time you save, you can easily earn the money to buy the better compass.

Avoid trying to learn compass use by rule-of-thumb methods. Some books attempt to make the problem too simple. Learn the logic of this chapter and you will be able to cope anywhere in the world, even in polar regions.

5

Grid references and route plans

Every point has a unique map reference. The whole of Britain is divided into squares with sides of 100 000m (109 400yd). Each of these large squares is identified by a pair of letters, NX for example. The small-scale Routefinder maps are further divided into squares of 10km (6 miles). Landranger and Pathfinder maps have squares with sides of 1km (0.6 miles).

To identify any of these kilometre squares – roughly the area of a village or a smallish loch – you need to combine those two letters with a four-figure grid reference. For example, NX 44 85 would adequately describe the position of Loch Enoch, a hill-loch about 2km (1 mile) east of The Merrick, in the Galloway Hills.

Before going any further you need to know which comes first, *eastings* or *northings*, because if you put the wrong one first you can be as much as 140km (87 miles) in error. Eastings, remember, are the numbered lines which run north and south, and you must count them from left to right – eastwards. Northings are similar lines across the map, and you must go from down to up – northwards. Eastings must be established before northings, and the easy way to remember is that E comes before N in the alphabet.

If you want to locate a village, a four-figure reference is good enough. For a field in the village, say a football field, you will need a six-figure reference, which gives an accuracy of 100m (330ft). For our purpose, the two letters of the British National Grid, or the map-sheet number, will put us in the right general area or range of hills, and a six-figure grid reference will be accurate enough for a summit, a church, a telephone kiosk, a pub or a Mountain Rescue Post.

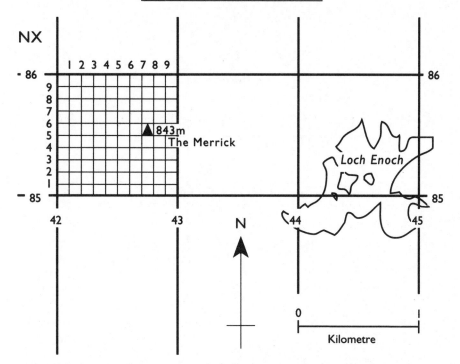

5.1 Split each kilometre square into 100 imaginary squares. The Loch Enoch square is NX 4485 and the Merrick trig point is NX 427855.

For a full example, let us return to the hills of 'Bonnie Gallowa' and refer to figure 5.1.

Imagine that every kilometre square is split by nine more east-ings and nine more northings, as shown in Square NX 42 85, to give another grid of 100 squares, each with sides representing 100m (330ft) on the ground. Remember that the particular square referred to is EAST of, and NORTH of the particular *intersection* of lines that we number.

For the summit triangulation pillar (concrete post) on top of The Merrick let us get the easting first: go east (left to right) past line 42, and past seven imaginary lines to give 42.7, or easting 427. For the northing, count north (bottom to top) past northing 85 and five imaginary northings to get 85.5 – northing 855. Check again, you must be right about this. Put the easting *before* the northing to give the full map reference of NX 427855.

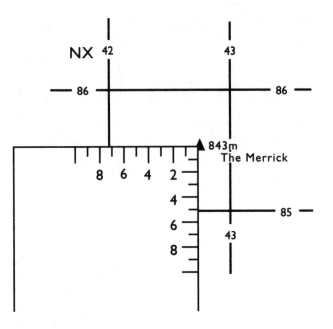

5.2 Using a Romer to pinpoint a summit. Ref: NX 427855.

To be really precise, use a *Romer* as shown in figure 5.2. One can be bought separately, but many compasses have Romers for the popular map scales etched onto their baseplates. You will probably find that guessing the grid reference is accurate enough. Romers just tend to be confused with the millimetre scale on the other edge of the baseplate.

Important grid references, on a rescue message, for example, should be double-checked. They should also be used with a description. 'The foot of Douglas Gap West Gully' or 'The bottom of Damnation' would probably be more use than a map reference on its own. Another idea is to send down a spare map accurately marked with a cross, which allows for the possibility that the person receiving the rescue message may not be conversant with map references.

Route plans

For a stroll in the park, a route plan is a bit superfluous, although it might be as well to tell someone where you are going, but a serious trip into wild country demands a bit of planning. If you make a plan, it is as well to write it down to check errors and omissions, and, if you have written it down, you can easily leave a copy with a responsible person. Thousands of rescue hours are used up in Britain every year searching for missing persons who have not left a route card. Time is also wasted on false alarms, so if you book out with a hut or hostel warden, or the police, make sure you phone them when you return.

We will presume you have decided to prepare a route plan. The most important compass bearings you will have to follow will be the ones you take from the summits of mountains. First, you have to confirm that you *are* on the true summit – but that is another story which we will come back to later. It is often quite easy to navigate to the top; except on complicated summit ridges, you merely go uphill until there is nothing higher. At the top your attention is distracted. People start chatting, eating and taking photographs. By definition, the summit is the most exposed place on the mountain, and you will probably get chilled very quickly. When you have spent 10 minutes on top everybody will be impatient to get going – not the time to take out your map and compass in the freezing gale and try to work out the most important bearing of the day – the descent route through a white-out. It is much better to prepare the whole thing in the comfort of your home or tent; have the bearings worked out and checked with variation added (subtracted for east variation, remember). Calculate your timings, and note all the distances. A suggested format for your route plan is shown in figure 5.3 overleaf. It is best to write on the same plan alternative routes you have considered, and possible escape routes. At least if you write them down it means you have given them some thought.

While on the subject of escape routes; wind direction is all important. It is all very well to get blown up a mountain with the

ROUTE PLAN

Date: _ _ _ _ _ _   Members of party: _ _ _ _ _ _ _ _ _ _ _ _ _

Weather forecast: _

Starting point reference: _ _ _ _ _   Description: _ _ _ _ _ _ _ _   Time: _ _ _ _ _

To:- grid reference	Description (of target)	Direction	Distance	Time (for distance)	Height gain	Time (for height gain)	Total time	Description (of route and terrain)	Possible alternative route	Escape route

Finish point reference: _ _ _ _ _ _   Estimated pick up time: _ _ _ _ _ _ _

Description: _ _ _ _ _ _ _ _ _ _   Estimated phone in time: _ _ _ _ _ _ _

5.3 Route plan – suggested format

wind on your tail, but consider that, if you do not attain the summit for any reason, you may be faced with a long descent *into* the wind. So plan your route with knowledge of the forecast wind direction and strength. Also remember that lee slopes for escape routes may be the most prone to windslab avalanches.

Timing is important. With experience and observation and, better, with local knowledge you will gain some idea. Remember that in the middle of a Scottish winter you may have only seven or eight hours of daylight, with 16 hours of darkness to survive if you get caught out with faulty torches or expired batteries. Generally, depending on whether you want to go fast or slow, and on your fitness, you should allow 15 or 20 minutes for every kilometre ($^5/_8$ mile) of horizontal distance, with steeper slopes taking longer. Timing is affected by ill-health, backpacking enormous loads, glacier lethargy, altitude and vagaries of terrain. Deep soft snow will really slow you down, even if you are wearing skis or snow-shoes, and deep heather is almost as bad. You have to reckon on scree slopes, impassable forests or spate rivers, long lines of crags, large and slushy peat hags on Bleaklow and Black Hill, horrible tussocks almost anywhere, and head-high bracken on bouldery slopes. For going up, the general rule is to add one minute for every contour line you cross if the contour (vertical) interval is 10m (33ft). We do not generally allow extra time for descending, although beginners often say that going down is harder than climbing. So, work out the time for the horizontal distance and add to it the time you have calculated for the height gain to find out the estimated total time.

We mentioned the importance of being sure that you are on the true summit. Taking the correct course down from the wrong peak can get you into a lot of trouble, as John Hinde explains.

'Chuck and I set off on a winter traverse of the Mamore Ridge in thick mist. Using the old 'one-inch' map, which did not show Na Gruagaichean clearly, we presumed we had reached the top. Our tatty map, not even protected by a polythene bag, was almost unreadable, especially at the fold. We had not bothered to check that there was a south-east peak, the highest, and a north-west summit, the one we had reached from Stob Coire a'Chairn. The two tops are separated by a steepish little dip. We blithely took a quick bearing, "Oh, its about north-east by the look of it", and headed off for what we thought was the continuation of the main ridge to the south peak of Binnein Mor. We quickly discovered that we were descending the north-east face of the north-west peak of Na Gruagaichean, which was about a grade 2 ice climb. We were capable and well equipped, and we weren't too enthralled with the weather, so we just carried on down and shortened our day. But if we had been novices, not wearing crampons or carrying ice-axes, the outcome might have been tragic.'

Navigating round

Summer hill-walking is completely different from doing the same routes under snow and ice, or on frozen turf. Most of the Scottish guide books describe the Munros (listed separate peaks over 915m/3000ft) and Corbetts (listed separate mountains between 915m and 762m (3000ft and 2500ft) under summer conditions. Planning winter walks, especially over the high plateaux, you may have to make allowances for avoiding snow cornices. For example, the plateau of Beinn a'Chaorainn above Glen Spean is often used as a training ground (figure 5.4). This is a fairly serious place, mainly because the curves of the corries look so innocuous on the map, luring people into trying to follow straight-line bearings from tops to summit, or vice versa. There are easy slopes to the west, but all the east face is steep and craggy. During the last few years there have been eight or nine separate instances of unroped walkers falling through cornices (overhanging eaves on the lee sides of ridges formed by the wind-saltation of snow particles) in poor visibility in this area. Even though in most cases there were no serious injuries, very steep falls of 200m (650ft), halted in soft snow halfway down the cliffs, have caused considerable retrieval problems for the rescuers.

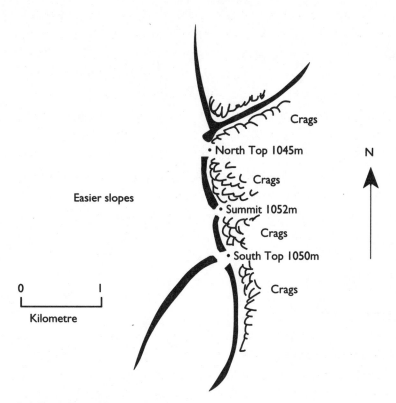

5.4 The ridges of Beinn a'Chaorainn.

One method of avoiding becoming a rescue statistic is to 'box' the corrie, as shown in figure 5.5 overleaf. If the South Top has been gained from Roughburn Bothy on the shore of Loch Laggan, and the visibility is poor, the first thing for the party to do is to rope up. Allow the first person plenty of rope, with the others following in single file tied within a few metres of each other. From your route plan you will know the straight-line bearing from the South Top to Beinn a'Chaorainn summit. It is probably about zero or 360 degrees magnetic. Find out the exact measurement yourself from the map. Add 270 degrees to the bearing and follow the course at a right angle, pacing out a safe distance – we would suggest at least 150m (490ft) – from the South Top. The number of double paces must be noted accurately. It is a bit like avoiding the

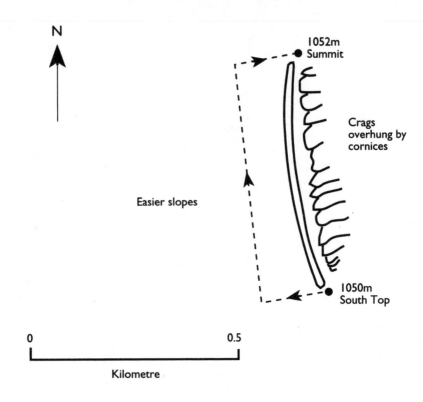

5.5 'Boxing' the corrie.

lake in Chapter 2, but the consequences of an error are worse. At the corner of your 'box' add 90 degrees and turn right on to your new course. Now pace out the exact straight-line distance (from your route card) which you have measured from the South Top to the summit. At the second corner add 90 degrees and turn right again.

Now we come to the real 'nitty-gritty'. In theory the summit is exactly 150m (490ft) ahead on the new course, but the leader may be a bit apprehensive approaching the cornice. It is a wise precaution to have a second rope tied to one of the anchor people and loosely held by the leader. In a white-out the rope can be thrown out ahead. If it can be seen lying level on the snow, at

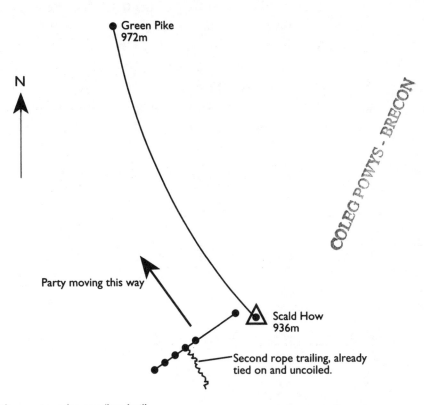

5.6 Using the cornice edge as a 'handrail'.

least you can see there is *something* in front.

The latest OS maps mark the spot height of the Centre Peak of Beinn a'Chaorainn as 1049m and the spot height is surrounded by a 1050 contour line. This is impossible of course, and the Ordnance Survey have admitted that the contour line is incorrect, but that the height of Beinn a'Chaorainn is in fact 1049m. Presumably, therefore, the new 'Munro' will now be the South Top at 1050m. The South Top is much easier to find in poor visibilty than the Centre Top; this may reduce the number of people walking through the cornice.

If the cornice edge can be vaguely distinguished – a variation of pale greys rather than a colour difference – it may be possible to use the edge of the plateau as a 'handrail' (page 87) to get from one top to another, as shown diagrammatically in figure 5.6 on the previous page. Movement will be very cautious, and the rope must be kept very tight – absolutely at right angles to the line of the cornice. You must be roped if close to an uncertain cornice, and at all costs avoid moving in single file *parallel* to the edge. If the cornice collapses you may all go down with it.

6

When theory meets the real world

'John Hinde was leading a party of seven hill-walking from a camp near Steall Ruins. For the summit of Ben Nevis, the weather was not too bad. It was snowing, but the breeze was only about 10 knots (18kph) from the south-west. There was a lot of snow lying but it was on a firm base, well consolidated. Everybody had proved reasonably fit, and although we had ascended through cloud for the final 500m (1640ft) we attained the summit in a little over three hours.

'Possibly the most difficult navigation in Britain is to navigate off the high plateaux, such as Nevis, Ben Alder and the Cairngorms, in winter. Great accuracy is required when the conditions make it harder to be precise and there are numerous instances of people falling though cornices.

'There was more snow than I thought, and the cloud was more dense. We were in a white-out. What were we to do? Follow the path? Which path? All traces were buried under 4m (13ft) of snow. Retrace our steps? Our footprints had been wiped out in just five minutes. Follow the cairns? Which cairns? Only the corrugated refuge which at that time topped the tower of the observatory ruins could be seen. The large Peace Cairn and even the triangulation pillar on its 3-m (10-ft) plinth were nowhere to be seen.

'The problem was how to navigate down the Tourist Track. Ian Clough's winter climbs guide book advised us to stay put in the last resort, or to follow the rim of the plateau to the top of the Red Burn. But most of the edge was corniced, with some of

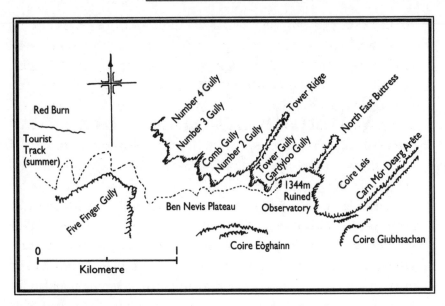

6.1 Ben Nevis.

the feathery edges sticking out 10m (33ft) over 500m (1640ft) drops. I did not wish to go too close to them.

'We needed to hit the zig-zags descending the West Flank and then we would be safe, but the tops of four gullies – Gardyloo, Tower, Number 2 and Comb Gully – lay across the direct bearing, all on the north edge of the plateau. A dog-leg course from the summit was needed. The first bearing south-west for exactly 150m (490ft) would ensure that we did not plummet through the cornices of Gardyloo or Tower Gullies. The second had to be very accurate (I made it 282 degrees grid +6 degrees west variation = 288 degrees magnetic) because the plateau narrowed about 800m (2600ft) ahead, with Number 3 Gully to the north (right) and Five Finger Gully to the left.

'The mountain has a history of people in a similar predicament just heading south. Some get away with it and survivors have said they went south because they knew the big crags were to the north and east. Unfortunately there are also crags of over

200m (650ft) just to the south at the head of Coire Eoghainn.

'It was easy leaving the summit. I just set my compass at 231 degrees (225 grid + 6 degrees west variation) from just east of the Observatory Ruin, allowing a little margin for error, and boldly paced out 98 double paces. I knew my natural step over level ground was 65 double paces for 100m (330ft); I had practised it so many times over accurately measured distances.

'Then we roped up. The other six tied close together, within 3m (10ft) of one another. I used all the rest of the rope to be way out in front. I wanted to ensure that if anybody fell through a cornice it would be only one of us. Also I needed the separation to concentrate on the navigation. My companions probably wondered why I took so much trouble. It was much easier to follow, as they could see me ahead. I could see nothing but whiteness – the snowfield, the falling flakes and the mist all merged into a blind world of white. I asked the others to do essential tasks. They all had to maintain strict single file, one counting the double paces up to each 100m (330ft) covered, another noting and shouting out the number of hundreds. One person with a stop-watch volunteered to do accurate timing. 'Tail-end-Charlie', on a bit more rope than the others, kept stopping to check the bearing, shouting any corrections.

'It was serious stuff, with a world of difference from blindfold games. I gained real admiration for those who are always blind yet show so much confidence. I walked much more slowly than usual, with many pauses, my eyes wide to try and penetrate the void, head sweeping from side to side. I had to try and remember to keep my compass away from the head of my ice-axe, my karabiners, my watch, my camera...

'After nearly 500m (1640ft) of nervous tension, 15 minutes of my hesitating grope, I spotted with instant relief a slight shadow hard across to my right, almost behind me. I recognized the shape of Number 2 Gully, with snow fronds of unbelievable delicacy reaching outwards. We still had to clear the top of Five Finger Gully, but that was not so nasty, and probably uncorniced. Now I had a fix, and a much wider angle of error could be tolerated. My second thoughts were of fear and disgust. I had come far too close to the top of Number 2, and I realized I should have made the first leg longer to ensure clearing it.

'Martin Moran has solved the problem much more effectively. He has published a book giving two distances and three bearings. However, you need to be pretty accurate judging the distances.

'How could I have regained the plateau if I had fallen though the cornice? With difficulty. My group would have held me for sure, but the rope would have dug deep into the overhang, and vast amounts of snow would have to be moved before I could climb back or be pulled up through the cornice. A second rope would have been helpful, and everybody versed in crevasse rescue technique.

'What did I learn from the adventure? Not to repeat it? I'm afraid not. Just two weeks later I was back on top of Nevis in very similar circumstances with another group. We did not stay long on the summit. Rather than face the stress of navigating down the Tourist Track in a white-out, I scuttled off back down the Carn Mor Dearg Arête before our tracks filled in.'

What other points are there? Don't listen if you are told the Ben is an easy mountain, least of all if the informant is one who benefits from the tourist trade. They all know that over 400 fell-runners race up and down it in early September, and that a Model T Ford car was driven to the top in 1911. They forget to mention that quite a few hard ice-climbers, having completed a serious route, fail to find the easy way off. Nobody in Britain seems to use the bamboo markers with orange surveyors' tape that we used on Mount McKinley – probably a good thing too, though it might be handy to have a roll of orange tape on rescue searches. Do-gooders who deface the mountains with piles of stones should remember that cairns are obliterated when they are really needed.

Don't believe guide books either. Many authors use maps with side edges not aligned north and south, perhaps to fit more map on to the page shape, perhaps for artistic effect. This is a dangerous practice. It is even worse if these maps go into print with no arrow indicating north. Such a map appeared in a 1969 Climbers' Guide to Ben Nevis. The Landranger 1:50 000 Series is adequate for most British mountains; but the latest OS Sheet 41 is not nearly detailed enough for navigation off Ben Nevis in a white-out. We recommend that you use a larger scale map. Other mountains have different problems, but the ruggedness of the Skye Cuillin also demands special maps.

On McKinley we rarely travelled without tents, sleeping bags, food, fuel and stoves. That was 30 years ago, but these days, in May, the peak climbing season, the Kahiltna Glacier is so heavily travelled by climbers attempting the West Buttress Route that a virtual trail leads to the summit. Skis, snowshoes and boots pack a trench into the snow as climbers avoid trail-breaking by following each other's footprints, and they mark the trail with wands. Heavy storms, however, knock down and bury the wands and fill in the trail. Landmarks vanish and a white-out ensues. Even with long hours of daylight, so different from Scotland in winter, tired climbers fail to find their tents, and are forced to dig snow caves, waiting for dawn without sleeping bags, foam pads, food or water. With temperatures dropping to -10°C (14°F), bivouacking in a snow cave and sharing body heat may prevent any serious hypothermia.

We recommend creating your own landmarks on glaciers and big snowfields, where white-outs can sweep in quickly, by placing wands every 55m (180ft) or so. Climbers should always travel roped up on a big glacier as protection against falling into a crevasse. Most teams use a 45-m (150-ft) rope. If the wands are spaced every 55m (180ft), the second climber can stay at a wand while the leader goes out to find the next. That way the team is never out of sight of a wand.

Aiming off and handrails

Glenn Randall writes of an experience in Argentina that taught him a lot about navigation in the real world.

'It was during a one-day, solo attempt on the summit of Aconcagua, at 6960m (22 834ft), the highest mountain in the Western Hemisphere. I started at 5800m (19 000ft), at the foot of the Polish Glacier, at 2 am. Thirteen hours later I was still 150m (490t) below the summit. A flu virus had stolen my voice, my muscles had become lard and a flotilla of black clouds was rolling in from the Pacific. I headed down.

'And not before time. It was nearly dark as I reached the broad snow bowl at the foot of the glacier. A few wands materialized out of the gloom, left by some previous expedition. They seemed to be leading too far to the right, or south, but I followed them anyway. I knew that just beyond the foot of the glacier was the top of a large cliff, with my camp below. I had walked around the north end of the cliff in the pre-dawn darkness 16 hours before. The cliff-top would act as a catching feature, alerting me that I needed to turn left, to the north, to begin my end-run around the cliff.

'I walked off snow onto rock and stumbled ahead. Suddenly an abyss yawned before me out of the darkness and flying snow. I had reached the cliff-top. The crux now was to find my way back through the complex, broken cliff bands that formed its north end.

'I began scrambling northward along the junction of snow and rock, thinking I was only minutes from my tent. But nothing looked familiar. The cliff shrank and petered out, but now I confronted a talus field studded with outcrops and small cliff bands. In darkness and storm, dehydrated and exhausted, I could not find the way back to my tent. I croaked "hello, anybody there?" a couple of times, but got no reply. I started thinking about digging a snow cave and waiting for dawn.

'Then, barely audible over the wind, I heard a voice, and stumbled in that direction. A tent appeared, occupied by some American climbers. They pointed me in the right direction, at last, and I soon found my tent only 300m (300yd) away. Too exhausted to eat the dinner my body desperately needed, I drank a quart of soup and collapsed into my sleeping bag.

'I made a serious mistake that almost cost me a forced bivouac on a sub-zero night at 5800m (19 000ft). I hadn't built a cairn, or series of cairns, to guide me around the cliff. After all, the weather had been perfectly clear when I started, and I expected to be back before dark – the oft-repeated refrain of lost hikers and climbers everywhere. In situations like that, it is best to plan for the worst case, not the best.

'But I had done some things right. I used a technique called "aiming off". Instead of aiming directly for the end of the cliff, I aimed to the right. Then, when I reached the edge of the glacier, I knew I had to turn left. If I had aimed directly for the cliff end and missed even slightly, I would have wasted even more time than I did wandering in the dark amidst the cliff bands and outcrops forming the cliff's indistinct end, wondering whether to go right or left.'

You can apply the same technique to following a bearing through the woods back to a road where you parked your car. It is impossible to follow a bearing with complete accuracy. If you miss by even a couple of hundred metres, your car may be hidden by a bend in the road and you won't know which way to turn. So, instead of aiming directly for the car, set your course about 10 degrees off. Then, when you hit the road, you know which way to turn.

The same principle applies in other situations: finding a bridge or ford across a river, a snow bridge across a lengthy crevasse, a camp you have placed along the shore of a large lake. Road, creek, crevasse and lake shore are all 'catching features': they tell you unmistakably that it is time to change course. Once you have made the turn, they can be considered as *handrails*. You can follow them without further reference to your map or compass. Thinking about those two concepts can often make your route-finding easier. Instead of heading cross-country for several kilometres, navigating through thick woods with a compass, it may well be easier to walk an extra 500m (1/4 mile) to a stream or lakeshore that runs parallel to your course and serves as a handrail. It will almost certainly be easier to walk that far to a track, than to beat through a plantation. Then look for a catching feature to tell you when to resume your original course. It might be a prominent side stream. It could also be a particular bearing on a prominent peak that you can see from the handrail.

It is all too easy, when you are travelling through the woods, to decide you have reached the feature you want to use as your handrail when you actually haven't. In fact, it is remarkably easy, if you are careless or in a hurry, to make the map seem to fit what you are looking at in any situation.

Don't bend the map!

John Hinde and a colleague had trained up some students and decided they were sufficiently knowledgeable to tackle a summer expedition unaccompanied, with very loose shadowing, in good weather. John Hinde takes up the story:

'The group included a couple of honours geography graduates – the worst, because they think they know about maps. Probably the best are the geologists, as they really have to know where they are doing practical fieldwork. This group used Sheet 33 of the 1:50 000 OS maps. They had walked from Kinbreack Bothy in Glen Kingie to Strathan at the head of Loch Arkaig, where they made an extraordinary mistake. There were two very deep and obvious glens draining into the loch. They were supposed to go upstream on the north bank of the first (River Dessarry) and walk about 15km (9 miles) across Mam na Cloiche-Airde to Sourlies Bothy on a west coast sea-loch (Loch Nevis).

'They crossed the Dessarry by a bridge, well shown on the map, and followed up the north bank of the River Pean. Once in the wrong glen they quite happily fitted the features they found to the features on the map without really checking; Glen Pean Bothy became Upper Glendessary. Then they walked off the map without knowing it – because they were about 5km (3 miles) too far south, but they were convinced that Lochan Leum an t-Sagairt was Lochan a'Mhaim.

'Even when they came to the deepest fresh-water loch in Britain (Loch Morar, over 300m/980ft deep) and found Oban Bothy, they thought they were at Sourlies. Oban was on the south shore of Morar, whereas Sourlies was on the north shore of Nevis. Ah well, perhaps the map was a bit out. Meanwhile my friend was nearly frantic. He was separated from the group by three sizeable rivers and a very rugged ridge of 670m (2200ft). Neither he nor I thought they could possibly have chosen the wrong glen in such good weather ...

'I should have known better. Years before that I had been a chief instructor responsible for training 39 students in the arts of mountaincraft, rescue procedures and so on. For five whole days on two expeditions my three instructors had taught them, and they had even practised going in groups of four to six without instructors. We landed them from the sail-training schooner *Captain Scott* at Kintail Lodge Hotel on Loch Duich (Map Sheet 33). Split into nine groups they had to walk 80km (50 miles) in three days to Roshven House on Loch Ailort.

'After about 9km (6 miles) of walking on the main road (A87), they headed south on a footpath over the south Cluanie Ridge. Their group discipline was very good. Instead of forming a crocodile they were well split up, with at least 15 minutes walk between the groups, each group out of sight of the others as they ascended a path beside the Allt Mhalagain. The weather was excellent. Their detailed and checked route cards, laboriously prepared on the messdeck the previous evening, reminded them what to do. Go up from the main road, cross the burn at the 70-m contour, then – after 2.5km (1½ miles) from the main road – recross the stream at a stream junction (at height 380m/1250ft), then steeply zig-zag up over the pass of the Black Slab (Bealach Duibh Leac 720m/2360ft).

'They did not know I was watching closely, ensconced on a

sun-warmed ledge high above them. I was surprised when the first group missed the zig-zag path and carried on beside the Allt Coire Toiteil. They followed a more obvious path, not marked on the map, heading towards a Munro called Sgurr na Sgine, but, having just crossed the burn at the proper junction, the correct pass was fairly obvious. I became incredulous when the second, and then the third, parties made the same error. I did nothing about it as there was no danger. The weather was settled high pressure, and they were well equipped with food and tents.

'After an hour or two of inactivity on my part, and disappointment that we had trained them so ineffectively, I began to think that most of them would go the wrong way. All the same it was hard to believe that every navigator of each group made the same mistake. Nine separate parties all went the wrong way. It was not just the responsibility of the leaders, because everybody was supposed to be checking and consulting, yet they followed like sheep. All the groups crossed a pass further west, and they all got back on the planned route at Kinloch Hourn eventually, but not before adding a couple of kilometres of rugged loch shore to their effort.'

What can we learn from that Kintail epic, apart from better group management and better instruction? The obvious point is that maps are not to be trusted for man-made features. Scottish maps are excellent on the whole, but they get a bit dated like everything else. We have seen new hydro-electric lochs marked on maps years before the dams have been completed, and coniferous plantations mapped before the planned trees have been planted, likewise with roads and buildings. But what cartographer could have predicted that a surge of Munro-baggers would tread out such a track? What *can* be trusted, with the reservations of granite quarries and nuclear bombs, are the shapes of the 'everlasting' hills. Within geological time the contours of the Highlands are reasonably static and a thoughtful interpretation of the contour lines would have guided those *Captain Scott* students over the correct col. The use of magnetic compasses was not needed because of the good visibility, but sometimes when people first learn to use compasses they tend to over-use them.

John Hinde tells how his wife and son got into trouble because they trusted a leader who relied on man-made features.

'It was winter in the Mediterranean, and they were members of the Cyprus Rambling Club on an outing. Twenty-five of them followed a man whose navigation was of the 'turn right at the next path junction, then second left' school. Their planned 10km (6 mile) walk probably doubled in length as they dragged on and on, and they were hopelessly lost when the sun set. They were in thorny, hilly country, somewhere near Amyrou Monastery 13km (8 miles) north of Limassol.

'Benightment wearing summer clothes with no spares can be quite pleasant in Cyprus in June – you just lie down and go to sleep – but in early March it can rain torrentially for days on end. The consequences of rain that night could have been dire, but they managed to get a fire going. The rescue services had been alerted by anxious relatives. A few of the RAF Mountain Rescue Team got their Landrovers to within a few kilometres – they even spotted the fire – but were unable to reach the ramblers that night. An RAF helicopter at long last lifted them all to safety. Fourteen-year-old Neil was delighted. He had always wanted a ride in a helicopter.'

Sometimes map and compass alone won't get you there. You have to use your head too.

That is good advice as well for correcting route-finding mistakes that have left you temporarily confused about your location. If you have been locating your position on the map periodically, and kept track of the direction you have been travelling, you cannot really become lost. All you need to do is backtrack to your last known location. Since there is always a possibility that you will need to reverse course – for many reasons beside getting lost – you should glance over your shoulder frequently to memorize what your route looks like when you are heading in the opposite direction.

If you have been following a bearing and think you should have reached your destination by now, but haven't, stop and analyse possible mistakes. Did you compensate for variation? Did you compensate in the right direction? Could you have overshot your destination? Or are you just moving more slowly than you thought, and it is still ahead? Often it pays to go to a nearby clearing or bare-topped knoll. The clear view may help you identify landmarks, Whatever you do, do not panic, and do not blunder off in some hastily chosen direction, compounding your confusion.

Following a stream downhill is *sometimes* good advice – for skiers lost near the Cairnwell, Braemar, for example, where the burns do not flow through great gorges. Elsewhere in the Highlands the advice would be lethal. There are numerous examples; if you try to get off Am Bodach (The Old Man, in the Mamore Forest) by following Allt (stream) Coire a'Mhail down northwards, you will get to the top of the very spectacular Steall Waterfall with no easy way off. In most places in the north and west Highlands, spate river crossings are a big danger. Even small burns become raging torrents, so if following one down make sure you do not get trapped in the *arrowheads* formed by tributaries. Some glens have only small burns on one side where the hill slopes are uniform, and a major tributary on the other side where a river from another glen joins the main river; so get on the best side from the watershed. Try and get local knowledge to find out where the serviceable bridges are located; some on the map are ruined and washed away.

If you are lost in cloud on a hillside, *stop*. Do not compound the error by wandering. Look at the map carefully and decide which kilometre square you are in. Even if you are really lost it is unlikely that you cannot locate yourself to one, or two, or even four squares. Then determine the important *aspect of slope*; stretch out both of your arms to the side exactly parallel to the contours when facing downhill. Take a bearing downhill at right angles to the contours. That is the aspect of slope. Look back at the map and you will find that there is probably only one place in your selected square, or even squares, where the slope matches, so you are well on the way to solving the problem. The main thing to do is think and not dash off. If you have splashed out the money for an altimeter, that will help as well.

When all else fails

If you are absolutely convinced that you cannot determine your location, and if you notified someone where you were going, and when you expected to be back, your best bet is to stay put and wait for searchers to find you. Nearly all wild areas in Britain are within the response area of a search-and-rescue organization. You will make their job easier if you can move to a nearby location that is easily visible from the air and the surrounding terrain – a ridgetop or some kind of clearing. Brightly coloured gear is easier to spot, or perhaps an orange survival bag held down with rocks. In mist, a rope fully stretched between cairns would be easier to find than persons lying asleep, or worse. Remember the mountain distress signal: six long whistle blasts, shouts, or torch flashes followed by one minute silence, repeated on and on. Keep blowing, shouting or flashing after you think the rescuers have found you, because they will be using your signals as homing bearings. These days, people have been found with CB radios or mobile phones, but that is something else. Such phones don't work in about 80 per cent of the terrain where you may get lost, but coverage will doubtless improve.

But all this doom-and-gloom stuff should happen to the other guy, not to you, provided you locate yourself on the map at the beginning of your trip, pinpoint your position periodically, and always know the direction in which you are travelling.

7

Altimeter navigation

In the golden age of alpine mountaineering, about 130 years ago, some climbers used scientific research as an excuse for going off to Europe and having a damned good time scaling the peaks. Often with guides to help them, they carried enormous mercury barometers and boiling-point thermometers to all the major summits, along with their bottles of Bouvier and legs of mutton. The instruments were to determine altitude. Unfortunately we no longer have the joy of exploration of the easier routes, but we do find it easier to determine the height. As well as the uplift cable stations and good maps we have dinky, accurate, but expensive altimeters, which are invaluable navigation aids. They may soon be superseded by the altimeters incorporated in some digital watches, or by satellite navigators. Who knows?

An altimeter gives you information about your location even when a compass is useless, except to take a bearing off the map. One glance at the altimeter gives you the height of the contour line you are on. If you have a second line of position – you know you are on a particular path, or following a particular stream or ridge crest – your position is pinpointed exactly. You are standing at the intersection of the contour line and the second line of position. Sometimes, particularly if you are following a path or ridge, your contour line will intersect twice. In that case, having even the vaguest idea of where you are (which side of the pass you are on, for example), should tell you your location exactly.

Figure 7.1 shows two examples. If your altimeter reads 300m (980ft) and you know you are on the path to Lochain a'Choire then you know you are at point A, where the 300-m contour line

94

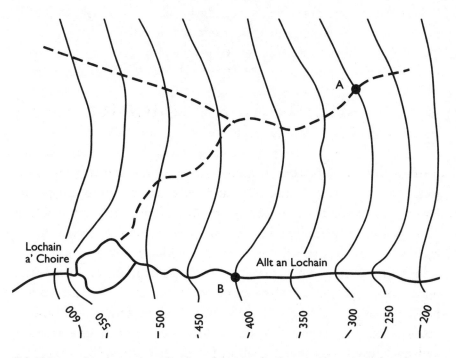

7.1 Using an altimeter and another line of position (such as a path or stream) to determine your position. N.B. Only thick (index) contours shown.

intersects the path. Since that contour line intersects the path only once, there can be no confusion. If it had intersected twice, you would have had to determine which of the two intersections marked your position by other means: the general lie of the land, the time spent walking and your estimate of your pace.

In the second example, let us say you are following up Allt an Lochain and your altimeter reads 400m (1300ft). You know you are at point B, where the burn intersects that contour. The same contour line never intersects a stream twice, of course, because streams always flow downhill.

The second line of position can also be a compass bearing. Perhaps you are in thick woods and get a glimpse of an identifiable peak. Or perhaps you are above the conifers in a storm and get a glimpse through a hole in the clouds of some identifiable pass. With a little luck, the compass bearing will cross the contour line indicated by your altimeter at something close to a right angle. If the bearing runs parallel to your contour line, all you have done is confirm your altimeter's reading. You can't pinpoint your position.

Mountaineers often find altimeters valuable even when a compass is useless and a map serves only to indicate the heights of the top and bottom of the climb. On a second ascent of Ghustung Himal North in 1965 John Hinde used an altimeter to keep track of his progress up a steep snow nose. Since he was making very little horizontal distance on the map, compass bearings couldn't pinpoint his position. The altimeter, however, let him gauge his rate of ascent and ration his effort accordingly. You can use the same principle to judge your progress up a hill. If you know from the map that the start is just above sea-level and the top is at 1344m (4409ft), you can take note of the time when you start and estimate your rate of ascent and time of arrival by how long it takes to climb the first 300m (980ft). If you start at 8 a.m. and take an hour to climb the first 300m (980ft), you can estimate you will take 4½ hours to climb to the top. In reality, with rest stops and fatigue, you will probably take a little longer.

In some situations, your compass and your altimeter can pinpoint your location even in a white-out. The key to this direction-of-slope method is using the compass to determine the bearing of an imaginary line pointing straight downhill. In the last chapter we called it the *aspect of slope*. Skiers call it the *fall line*. By definition, that line will be perpendicular to the contour line (determined by your altimeter) on which your position lies. Take a look at figure 7.2. If your altimeter tells you that you are on the 1050m contour, for example, and your aspect-of-slope line runs at a bearing of 160 degrees grid – you know you must be at position A. If the bearing is 230 degrees grid you know your location must be position B.

This method won't help you everywhere, obviously. You cannot determine your position on a broad hillside resembling a tilted tabletop, for example. But use of this method would have saved a bit of effort and exposure to danger when John Hinde was ascending Derry Cairngorm with a friend in thick mist.

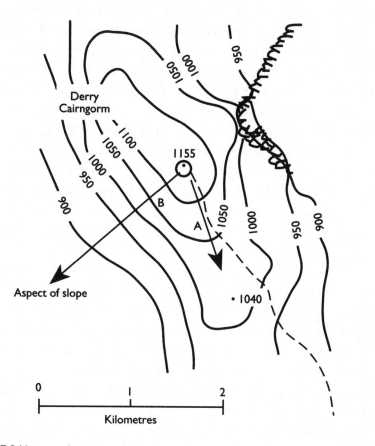

7.2 Using an altimeter and the aspect-of-slope method to determine your position.

'We had walked from Derry Lodge and put on skis near the summit of Carn Crom. The dotted line on figure 7.2 shows the route we should have taken. When we reached point A, we more or less continued on the same bearing, contouring round on the 1050m (3445ft) level until we reached point B. When we finally turned uphill, we found ourselves forced to switchback repeatedly, an exhausting and tedious process. Also the steep slope, unlike the gentler ridge we should have been on, was prone to avalanche. A quick map check would have saved both energy and nail biting.'

In all the techniques just described, the accuracy of your position estimate depends on the accuracy of your altimeter. Altimeters vary widely in accuracy, with really good ones costing £120 or so. The accuracy of an altimeter also depends, to a degree, on the user. To maximize its usefulness, and correct possible errors, you need to know a little about how altimeters work.

Altimeters are closely related to barometers. Both work by measuring air pressure: in effect, the weight of a column of air rising above the instrument's position. The higher you go, the less atmosphere lies above you. Altimeters translate that pressure drop into an altitude reading.

Pocket altimeters use a small, sealed metal capsule to sense air pressure. Most of the air inside the capsule is removed during manufacturing, so a partial vacuum exists. As the pressure outside the capsule varies, the walls of the capsule flex in and out. Those movements, which are maybe only a fraction of a millimetre, are translated via a complex mechanism to the movements of a pointer, which rotates around a dial to indicate the altitude. The dial can be adjusted in relation to the pointer, which allows you to correct errors by setting the altimeter to the proper altitude. If you arrive at a loch that the map tells you is at 1000m (3280ft), for example, and your altimeter tells you it is at 1050m (3440ft), you can adjust the altimeter back down to the correct reading of 1000. On most altimeters, the pointer also indicates the pressure directly, so the instrument functions as a barometer.

All metals expand and contract as the temperature fluctuates. Inexpensive altimeters cannot compensate for that, which means that a change in their temperature causes them to register an apparent change in altitude even when the instrument is stationary and the pressure unvarying. Using an inexpensive altimeter that is not temperature-compensated can lead to errors of as much as 200m (650ft) if you take the instrument out of a warm pocket and let it chill to ambient temperature on a wintry day. To minimize such errors, let the altimeter adjust to the prevailing temperature before setting it to your starting altitude. Then keep the altimeter in an outside pocket of your pack, so it remains at approximately the same temperature.

Better instruments incorporate some element in their design which counteracts the effect of instrument temperature. It is usually a strip made of two metals, fused together, that have widely different rates of expansion and contraction when heated or cooled. When the strip is heated, for example, the strip bends away from the metal that expands the fastest. That bending is used to counteract expansion in other parts of the instrument that would otherwise lead to an apparent change in altitude.

The first source of error, therefore, can be greatly reduced simply by buying a high-quality, temperature-compensated instrument. The second source of error must be controlled by the user.

The second error arises because air pressure fluctuates constantly, even at the same altitude, as the weather changes. If you are moving at the same time, it is impossible to sort out the two influences on your altimeter. The only solution is to reset your altimeter at known heights – a pass, a lake, a summit, the point where a path crosses a stream or cuts across a prominent ridge. If you can reset your altimeter every hour or so, you can limit the error due to weather to 10m (33ft) or less – usually less.

Larger errors due to weather are common when you camp somewhere for a day or longer. If there is a major weather change during the night, for example, the difference between evening and morning readings can easily be a 100m (330ft) or more. If you know the exact altitude of your camp from the map, you can correct as you normally would. If you cannot determine your height above sea-level from the map, the best way to maintain the accuracy of your altimeter readings is to note the reading when you arrive in camp, then reset the altimeter to that reading when you leave.

The easiest way to correct for both possible errors in your altimeter is simply to reset it at known altitude points as frequently as possible. With less effort than it takes to sight a single landmark and plot the bearing on the map, your altimeter will then serve you well as a navigational tool.

8

The sport of orienteering

No sooner do some master a skill than they feel the need to test their mastery in competition with others. When such people combined map and compass skills with cross-country running, the sport of orienteering was born. It began in Sweden in 1918, and was introduced to Britain in the early 1960s. In Sweden, Norway and other European countries, orienteering is a national pastime. A single big meet in Sweden can pull in as many as 20 000 enthusiasts.

In the most popular form of orienteering, competitors must find, in the correct order, a series of 6 to 30 control points hidden in the woods. A red and white prism-shaped structure made of fabric or cardboard marks the control point. The controls, as they are called, are either marked on the map furnished to each participant at the start of the race, or copied by the participant from a master map after the starting gun sounds. There is a code number or letter at the control, and a pin-punch for competitors to mark their cards to prove they have visited. Easy courses might be only 2.5km (1½ miles) long; expert courses might extend for 13km (8 miles). The winner is the runner who finishes in the shortest time after locating all the controls. Runners who miss a control are disqualified. Orienteering features extensively on Outward Bound courses. The controls may be semi-permanently sited and only changed if paths begin to develop.

Orienteering maps are usually drawn to a larger scale than most OS maps. A scale of 1:10 000 is common, with north/south lines perhaps 250m (820ft) apart. On 1:15 000 maps the separation between north/south lines could be 500m (1640ft). The top of the map always represents magnetic north instead of geographic north, so there is no need to worry about correcting for variation. Meet officials field-check each map as they plot the course and place the controls. They delete paths that have vanished, mark any new ones, and add the details that are one key to finding the controls: fences, boulders, knolls, tiny streams that would escape the notice of the Ordnance Survey. In addition to the map, runners get a very brief description of the terrain feature at which each control point will be found.

Orienteering races always use a staggered start, so runners cannot simply follow each other from control to control. Ideally, the controls are also placed so that runners approaching a particular control get no clues from others leaving it.

Only in beginners' races will a straight-line compass course ever be the fastest way from one control to the next. Victory doesn't necessarily go to the fastest runner. Instead, it goes to the competitor who can visualize the best route from a rapid study of the map, then follow it quickly and accurately. Expert orienteers use many of the techniques described elsewhere in this book, which in fact originated in the sport. Wherever possible, for example, they look for handrails that lead them in the right direction. Paths and roads are the most obvious handrails; power lines, fences, streams and edges of fields are less obvious but equally effective. Over a short distance, the sun can be a handrail. Perhaps you can follow your shadow, or run with the sun full in your face. Or perhaps you can tell from the map that you need to follow a course that crosses the shadows thrown by trees at a 90-degree angle. With a good handrail as a guide, a runner can move out at full speed without wasting time checking map and compass.

As runners near the control, they begin searching for a catching feature crossing their path at 90 degrees to alert them to slow down and begin navigating more carefully. A catching feature can be any of the features described as potential handrails. Once runners locate the intersection of the handrail and the catching feature,they begin searching for the attack point: some relatively easy-to-follow landmark close to the control. From there, runners follow a precise compass bearing for a distance measured off the map. To keep track of distance, they measure the length of their stride beforehand and then count paces until they locate the control.

Good route-finding involves more than identifying handrails, catching features and attack points. It also involves decisions about dealing with obstacles like hills, forests and brush: over, around or through?

As a rule of thumb, every metre of height gain takes as much time as running 12.5m (40ft) on the level. If your map's contour interval is 5m (16ft), then climbing one contour interval takes as much time as running 62.5m (200ft) on the level (or a 20ft contour is equivalent to 250ft). You can use this rule of thumb to estimate whether it is faster to go over or around a hill. Let us say going over the hill involves a climb of four contour intervals or the equivalent of 250m (820ft) of horizontal travel, plus 100m (330ft) of actual horizontal travel as measured on the map. The total is 350m (1150ft). If going around the hill takes less than 350m (1150ft) of running, it is faster to go around. If it takes more than 350m (1150ft), go over the top.

Another rule of thumb concerns the extra time required to run through vegetation and brush. Let us say it takes one unit of time for you to cover 100m (330ft) on a good path or road. You can then estimate that it will take you two units of time to cover the same distance through tall grass, three units of time through forest with light undergrowth and four to six units of time through very heavy undergrowth.

If the idea of honing your route-finding skills by finding controls appeals to you, but you don't like the competitive aspect, you can attend nearly all meets and amble through the course (or a different one set up especially for people like you) at your own pace, locating the controls and checking them off your list. In orienteering jargon, you will be known as a *wayfarer* or *map-walker*. Non-competitive orienteering is especially popular among families with small children.

Want to know more? Write to the British Orienteering Federation National Office: 'Riversdale', Dale Road North, Darley Dale, Matlock, Derbyshire, DE4 2HX.

There is a 24-hour phone answer service on 0629 733769. *Compass Sport* is Britain's national orienteering magazine.

Index